The Adventures of Tom Sawyer

by Mark Twain

Level 2
(1300-word)

Adapted by David Thayne

JN250438

IBC パブリッシング

はじめに

　ラダーシリーズは、「はしご (ladder)」を使って一歩一歩上を目指すように、学習者の実力に合わせ、無理なくステップアップできるよう開発された英文リーダーのシリーズです。

　リーディング力をつけるためには、繰り返したくさん読むこと、いわゆる「多読」がもっとも効果的な学習法であると言われています。多読では、「1.速く 2.訳さず英語のまま 3.なるべく辞書を使わず」に読むことが大切です。スピードを計るなど、速く読むよう心がけましょう（たとえば TOEIC® テストの音声スピードはおよそ 1 分間に 150語です）。そして一語ずつ訳すのではなく、英語を英語のまま理解するくせをつけるようにします。こうして読み続けるうちに語感がついてきて、だんだんと英語が理解できるようになるのです。まずは、ラダーシリーズの中からあなたのレベルに合った本を選び、少しずつ英文に慣れ親しんでください。たくさんの本を手にとるうちに、英文書がすらすら読めるようになってくるはずです。

English Conversational Ability Test
国際英語会話能力検定

● **E-CATとは…**
英語が話せるようになるための
テストです。インターネット
ベースで、30分であなたの発
話力をチェックします。

● **iTEP®とは…**
世界各国の企業、政府機関、アメリカの大学
300校以上が、英語能力判定テストとして採用。
オンラインによる90分のテストで文法、リー
ディング、リスニング、ライティング、スピー
キングの5技能をスコア化。iTEP®は、留学、就
職、海外赴任などに必要な、世界に通用する英
語力を総合的に評価する画期的なテストです。

www.ecatexam.com

www.itepexamjapan.com

《本シリーズの特徴》

• 中学校レベルから中級者レベルまで5段階に分かれています。自分
に合ったレベルからスタートしてください。

• クラシックから現代文学、ノンフィクション、ビジネスと幅広いジャ
ンルを扱っています。あなたの興味に合わせてタイトルを選べます。

• 巻末のワードリストで、いつでもどこでも単語の意味を確認できま
す。レベル1、2では、文中の全ての単語が、レベル3以上は中学
校レベル外の単語が掲載されています。

• カバーにヘッドホーンマークのついているタイトルは、オーディオ・
サポートがあります。ウェブから購入／ダウンロードし、リスニン
グ教材としても併用できます。

《使用語彙について》

レベル1：中学校で学習する単語約1000語

レベル2：レベル1の単語＋使用頻度の高い単語約300語

レベル3：レベル1の単語＋使用頻度の高い単語約600語

レベル4：レベル1の単語＋使用頻度の高い単語約1000語

レベル5：語彙制限なし

読みはじめる前に

　本書で使われている用語です。わからない語は巻末の
ワードリストで確認しましょう。

- [ ] adventure
- [ ] beard
- [ ] beetle
- [ ] cart
- [ ] cave
- [ ] farm
- [ ] forest
- [ ] ghost
- [ ] graveyard
- [ ] jail
- [ ] leader
- [ ] meeting-house
- [ ] pirate
- [ ] prison
- [ ] river-bank
- [ ] spirit
- [ ] storm
- [ ] woods

登場人物

Tom Sawyer トム・ソーヤー　いたずらと冒険が大好きな少年。両親を亡くし、弟のシッド、いとこのメアリーとともにポリーおばさんのもとで暮らしている。

Huckleberry Finn ハックルベリー・フィン　通称ハック。学校に行かず、自由きままに暮らす。トムの相棒。

Becky Thatcher ベッキー・サッチャー　トムの同級生の少女。トムはベッキーのことが大好き。

Aunt Polly ポリーおばさん　トムのおば。いたずらっ子のトムに手を焼きながらも、かわいがっている。

Sid シッド　トムの弟。トムとは正反対の性格で、おとなしく、いたずらや冒険が好きではない。

Mary メアリー　ポリーおばさんの娘で、トムの年上のいとこ。まじめで、トムの世話をやく。

Joe Harper ジョー・ハーバー　トムの学校の友だち。トム、ハックと冒険に明け暮れる。

Indian Joe インジャン・ジョー　町の荒くれ者。ある日事件を起こしてしまう。

Muff Potter マフ・ポッター　いつも酔っ払っている老人。事件の容疑者となる。

CONTENTS

Teacher　　Aunt Polly　　Mary

Sid　　Tom　　Huck

Muff Potter   Indian Joe

Joe   Becky   Mr. Thatcher

A Few Words to Begin

Most of the stories in this book really happened.

One or two stories are my own and others happened to boys in my school. Huck Finn was a real boy and Tom Sawyer is made from three real boys.

My book is for boys and girls, but I hope that men and women also will read it. I hope that it will help them to remember when they were boys and girls, and how they felt and thought and talked, what they believed, and the strange things they sometimes did.

MARK TWAIN
Connecticut,USA 1876

1

Tom Gets into Trouble with Aunt Polly

"Tom! When I find you, I'll—"

The old lady looked for the boy. She looked under the bed, but only the cat came out. She looked out of the door, and saw the boy running through the garden.

"You, Tom! What are you doing?"

"Nothing."

"Nothing! What's that on your face?"

"I don't know, Aunt Polly."

"Candy! I told you not to eat candy." Aunt Polly was about to hit the boy when he shouted.

"Look!"

The old lady turned and the boy ran. He quickly ran through the garden and was gone.

Aunt Polly smiled.

"That boy! I didn't want to hit him, but if he doesn't go to school, I'll make him work on Saturday. He's my dead sister's son, so I want him to be a good boy."

Tom didn't go to school. He had a fun day and got home late. In the evening he did his homework. Sid, his brother, had already finished. Sid was a quiet boy who never got into trouble.

At dinner, his Aunt Polly asked Tom about his afternoon.

"Tom, was it warm in school?"

"Yes, Aunt Polly."

"Did you want to go swimming?"

"No, not really." Tom knew his aunt knew he hadn't been to school.

She touched his shirt. It was dry. But Tom knew what she would touch next. "We put water on our heads to cool down," he said quickly.

She believed him. She wanted to believe him.

The summer evenings were long. Tom walked

along the street. He stopped when he saw a stranger, a boy a little taller than himself.

He was dressed in nice clothes and shoes.

The two boys looked at each other. When one moved, the other moved. They walked around each other, eye to eye.

"If we fight I can win!" Tom said.

"Try it."

"I can."

"No, you can't."

"I can."

"You can't."

"Can!"

"Can't!"

Then Tom said, "I could win with one hand."

"Go ahead and try."

"You're afraid."

They moved closer. Then they started pushing and suddenly they were on the ground, hitting and fighting.

Tom got on top and hit the other boy hard.

"Give up."

The boy was crying.

"Had enough?!"

"Enough!" said the boy. Tom let him get up and walk away.

But when Tom turned to leave, the boy hit him with a rock. Tom ran after the boy, who ran to his home. His mother came out and told Tom to go home.

Tom got home late, and so he quietly entered through a window. But Aunt Polly was waiting for him. Sid had told her everything. Tom would have to work on Saturday.

"Let's go swimming. Or do you want to work?" Ben asked.

"What do you mean, work?" Tom said. "Maybe it's work and maybe it's not. But I like it."

"You like it?"

"Of course. You don't get to paint a fence every day."

Ben stopped eating his apple. Tom continued painting and then stopped to look at his work.

"Tom, let me paint a little," Ben said.

Tom thought and then said, "No, not this fence. You could help paint the back fence, but not this one."

"Let me try. Please. I'll be careful. I'll give you some of my apple."

"No, Ben."

"I'll give you all of my apple!"

Tom gave the brush to Ben. While Ben painted in the hot sun, Tom sat under a tree eating the apple.

Other boys came along; Bill and John. They stopped to laugh, but soon they were painting too. Each one had to give Tom a toy or something to paint. In a few hours, Tom felt rich.

He didn't do anything, but the fence had been painted three times. If he had more paint, Tom would have been even richer.

Tom had learned an important thing. Work and play are the same thing. But you have to work before you can play.

3

Tom is Happy and Sad

Aunt Polly was sitting by the window. She was sleeping and holding the cat.

"May I go and play now, Aunt Polly?" Tom asked.

"Have you finished already?"

"Yes."

"Is that true, Tom? It makes me sad when you lie."

She was surprised when she saw the fence.

"You do know how to work! Go and play now." She gave Tom a large apple, but didn't see him take a piece of cake too.

Tom ran to the village. Two groups of boys had met for a fight. Tom was the leader of one group and Joe Harper the leader of the other. But Tom and Joe didn't fight. They sat together and gave orders.

When the fight was finished, they agreed to fight again on another day. Tom started to walk home alone. At Jeff Thatcher's house he saw a girl in the garden. She had blue eyes and yellow hair. Tom used to have a girlfriend called Amy Lawrence, but not any more.

He watched until the girl looked at him, and began to jump around and walk on his hands so she would watch him more. She just walked into the house, but first she threw a flower to him.

Tom picked up the flower and put it under his shirt, near his heart.

He sat there until it got dark.

Aunt Polly thought Tom looked happy.

Later that evening, Sid, his brother, took some candy without asking. But Aunt Polly didn't believe that Sid could be bad, so she hit Tom. Later she learned she was wrong and felt sorry, but she didn't say sorry to Tom.

Tom felt very sad. He thought about dying. Then she would be sorry.

During the night he went to the river. Maybe he would kill himself in the river. Then he remembered his flower and took it out. Would the girl be sad if he died? This thought made him happy.

On his way home he passed the Thatcher's house. There was a light on in a window. Was it her room? He sat under the window holding her flower. He would sit there and die in the cold. In the morning, she would look out the window and see him.

Suddenly the window opened. Someone threw water out the window and it fell on him.

Tom jumped up and ran away.

Sid saw his brother coming in. Tom's wild eyes made Sid too afraid to speak. But he would tell his aunt.

4
Going to Sunday School

It was a sunny Sunday morning. Tom was learning some words from the Bible. Sid had already finished, but Tom was slow. He was thinking about other things.

Tom was learning five verses. Some were long and some short. Tom had found five short ones. Aunt Polly's daughter, Mary, helped him learn them so he could say them without looking at the book.

Mary gave him a pen for studying as well. It was not a good pen, but it was a pen. Tom was pleased.

Then Mary helped him put on his Sunday clothes. He hoped that she would forget his shoes. But she did not.

When they were ready, the three children went to Sunday school. Mary and Sid enjoyed Sunday school, but Tom did not want to go.

At the church door Tom stopped to speak to a friend. "Billy, do you have a yellow ticket?"

"Yes."

"Will you sell it to me?"

"What will you give me for it?"

Tom bought Billy's yellow ticket. Then Tom stopped other boys, and bought more tickets, some red and some blue. After ten minutes he went into the church.

These tickets were given for learning the Bible verses. A blue ticket was given for two. A red ticket for 20. A yellow ticket for 200. If a student learned two thousand verses, and got ten yellow tickets, the Sunday-school teacher gave the student a Bible.

It was a wonderful day when a boy or a girl received a Bible. Tom did not want the Bible. But he did want the wonderful experience of receiving it.

"Now, children," the teacher said, "sit quietly, and listen, like good boys and girls."

While the teacher was talking, three men, a lady and a girl entered the church. Tom was very happy to see the girl. He began fighting with the other boys, so the new girl would look at him and smile.

He quickly forgot the woman who threw water on him the night before.

The men and lady sat at the front of the church.

One man was Jeff Thatcher who lived in the village. Another man was his brother, the great Mr. Thatcher. He had traveled around the world and lived in the next large town.

The teacher wanted to give a Bible to a boy or girl today, so the famous Mr. Thatcher would know that this was a fine Sunday school. But no child had enough yellow tickets.

Suddenly Tom Sawyer stood up. He had nine yellow tickets, nine red tickets, and ten blue tickets. The teacher was surprised Tom had so many tickets. He did not believe that Tom had learned two thousand verses. He did not believe that Tom had learned twelve.

The other boys watched Tom. Everyone wished they had enough tickets for a Bible.

Some boys were angry, because they had sold their tickets to Tom. He had become so rich from letting them paint the fence, he could buy their Sunday school tickets.

Now they knew they had been silly.

Tom stood next to the famous Mr. Thatcher. He put his hand on Tom's head and called him a fine little man. Tom could not speak. This was because he was a great man, but also because he was her father.

The famous Mr. Thatcher asked, "What is your name?"

"Tom."

"Is that all?"

"Thomas."

"But you have more? Another name?"

"Tell the man your other name, Thomas," said the teacher.

"Thomas Sawyer."

"You are a very good boy. Two thousand verses is a lot. And you will always be happy that you learned them. Learning makes great men and good men. You will be a great man and a good man some day, Thomas. You will remember this day and be glad that you went to Sunday school. Now, Thomas, tell me and this lady some of the Bible verses you have learned. Now, you know the names of the twelve great friends of Jesus Christ. Tell us the names of the first two."

Tom's face became red. He looked down at his feet and said nothing.

The teacher knew Tom could not answer. But Tom felt that he must speak.

"Can you tell me," said the lady.

Tom remembered two names from the Bible. He did not remember who the people were or what they had done. But the two names were always together. He shouted them now:

"DAVID AND GOLIATH!"

But David and Goliath were not friends of Jesus

Christ. They were in a different Bible story, and David had killed Goliath.

Let's finish this story about Tom Sawyer in Sunday school.

5

In Church

In church the people came to hear Mr. Sprague speak to them. Mr. Sprague spoke and prayed in church every Sunday.

The Sunday school children sat with their fathers and mothers. Aunt Polly sat with Tom, Sid and Mary. Aunt Polly made Tom sit far from the window and the interesting things outside.

Other people came in and sat down. There were old, young, rich and poor people. There was Mrs.

Douglas, whose husband had died. She was rich and kind, and she lived in the big house on Cardiff Hill. There was Willie, the "Good Boy" of the village. He came to church with his mother. All the other mothers talked of his goodness. All the other boys did not like him.

The church became quiet.

They began with a song. Then Mr. Sprague prayed for many things and for many people. He prayed for the church, and little children, and other churches in the village, and then for the village, the country, and last, for people in far countries.

Tom did not enjoy hearing Mr. Sprague pray, but he knew he must be quiet.

While Mr. Sprague prayed, a flying beetle stopped on the back of the seat in front of Tom. The beetle began to clean its body. The beetle knew it was safe. Tom was afraid to touch the beetle while Mr. Sprague was praying, in case something bad happened to him. But as Mr. Sprague finished praying, Tom picked up the beetle. But his aunt saw this. She told him to let the beetle fly away.

Then Mr. Sprague began a longer talk. Tom began to count the pages as he talked. After church, Tom always knew how many pages there had been. But usually, he didn't know what had been said.

But this morning Tom was interested. Mr. Sprague talked about future peace in the world. Strong and weak countries would be friends. The strong countries, he said, would be like a strong, forest animal. The weak countries would be like a weak farm animal. But they would all be friends, and so kind that a little child could lead them.

Tom wanted to be that child.

Then the animal stories stopped and Tom lost interest. He remembered he had a large black beetle in a small box in his pocket. As he took the beetle out of his pocket, it hurt Tom's finger. It hurt and he dropped the beetle on the floor.

Tom put his finger in his mouth.

The beetle fell on its back, moving its legs. Tom watched it. Other people, also not interested in Mr.

Sprague's talk, watched the beetle.

Then a sad dog entered the church looking for something interesting to do. He saw the large black beetle. This looked interesting and he became happy. He walked to the beetle and touched it with his nose. Suddenly the beetle hurt the dog's nose and the dog cried loudly.

The beetle fell on the floor, again on its back.

People who saw this laughed quietly. Tom was very happy. The dog felt silly and was angry. He played with the beetle for a while and then found a smaller beetle to play with. The tired dog forgot about the large black beetle and sat on it.

Again the beetle hurt the dog, but did not let go. Crying, the dog ran around the church. The cries became louder and louder, until the owner threw the dog out of a church window. The dog ran away.

Everyone who saw this laughed quietly.

Mr. Sprague had stopped speaking. He began again, but it was difficult. People were still laughing. Everyone was happy when it was time to go home. Tom was happy. It was good when something different happened in church. He was happy to let the dog play with his beetle. But the dog should not have run away with it.

6
A Talk of Devils—Happy Hours

The next morning Tom was very sad. It was the start of another week of school. He usually began this day wishing that there had been no Saturday and no Sunday.

He sat on his bed, thinking. If he were sick, he could stay home. He thought about his body, but he could not find a sick part.

Then he looked at his foot. His foot had been hurt.

He had an idea. He began to cry as if with pain.

But Sid continued to sleep.

Tom's voice grew louder. Now he thought the pain in his foot was real.

Still Sid did not wake up.

"Sid, Sid!" he shouted.

Sid sat up and looked at him. "Tom! What is wrong?"

No answer.

Sid shouted again.

Tom said, "Oh, don't do that, Sid. It hurts me."

"I must call Aunt Polly."

"No. Don't call her." He cried loudly again. Then he said, "I will forget everything bad that you have done to me, Sid. When I am dead—"

"Oh, Tom, are you dying?"

"Give my cat with one eye to that new girl, and tell her—"

But Sid was gone. He ran to his aunt. "Oh, Aunt Polly! Tom is dying!"

"Dying? I can't believe it!"

But she ran to Tom's bed, "Tom! Tom, what is wrong?"

"It's my foot, Aunt. It hurts. The doctor must cut it off."

The old lady sat down in a chair and laughed, then cried and then did both together. Then she said, "Tom, you stop that, and get out of bed."

Tom stopped crying and the pain stopped too.

As he walked to school, he met Huckleberry Finn. Huckleberry's father was always drunk. The mothers in the village did not like Huckleberry. But all the children liked him. Everyone wanted to be like him.

Tom also wished he could be like Huckleberry. He had been told never to play with Huckleberry, so he played with him as much as he could.

Huckleberry always wore old clothes that were too big for him. His hat was full of holes. His coat touched the ground. He went any place he wished. He did not sleep in a bed; he did not sleep in a house. He did not go to school or to church. He could go swimming or fishing when and where he wanted. He was the first boy to wear no shoes in the early summer. He was the last boy to wear shoes in the early winter. He never washed.

He had everything that any boy could want.

Tom said, "Hello, Huckleberry."

"Hello yourself."

"What is that?"

"Dead cat."

"Let me see, Huck. Where did you get him?"

"From a boy."

"Why do you want a dead cat, Huck?"

"To take off these warts." Huckleberry showed Tom the hard bits of skin on his hands.

"Huck, when are you going to do it?"

"Tonight. I think that they will come to get old Williams tonight."

"But they put him in the ground Saturday. The devils would take him Saturday night."

"The devils can't come until twelve. At twelve on Saturday night, it is Sunday. Devils can't come on Sunday."

"I never thought of that. Let me go with you."

"If you won't be afraid."

"Afraid! Will you come to my house and call to me? Make a sound like a cat."

"Yes. But you must answer. Another night I came to your house, and made a sound like a cat. But you never answered. And your neighbor threw rocks at me."

"Aunt Polly was watching me. But I will answer this time."

Tom quickly walked to school and sat in his seat.

The teacher looked at him. "Thomas Sawyer!"

Tom knew that trouble was coming when his full name was used.

"Why are you late again?"

Tom looked around the room. He saw the new girl. No one was sitting next to her.

He said, "I STOPPED TO TALK WITH HUCKLEBERRY FINN."

Everyone was surprised.

25

"Thomas Sawyer, I never heard more surprising words. Take off your coat." The teacher hit him, "Go and sit with the girls!"

The new girl turned her back towards Tom. When she turned toward him, she saw an apple on the table in front of her. She moved it away. Tom moved it toward her. She moved it away again. Tom returned it. She did not move it again.

Tom began to draw a picture on a piece of paper. She tried to see it and said, "Let me see."

He showed her. It was a picture of a house. It was not good, but she thought that it was. "It is nice. Now make a man."

The man was bigger than the house.

"It is beautiful. Now make me."

He made a picture of another person.

"That is very nice. I wish I could make pictures."

"I will teach you. At noon. Do you go home to eat?"

"I will stay if you stay."

"Good. What is your name?"

"Becky Thatcher. What is yours? Oh, I know. It is Thomas Sawyer."

"That is my name when I am bad. I am Tom when I am good. Please call me Tom."

Next Tom began writing something. She asked to see.

"No. You will tell what it is."

"I promise never to tell."

Tom let her pull the writing away. She read these words: "I love you."

27

"Oh, you bad thing!" And she hit his hand. But her face looked happy.

Suddenly he felt a hand on his ear, pulling him from the seat. He moved back to his normal seat. Everyone laughed.

Tom's ear hurt, but his heart was happy.

7
A Plan is Made

At noon Tom ran to Becky and said quietly:

"Start to go home with the others, and then return here. I will do the same."

Soon both had returned. Alone in the school, Tom showed Becky how to make a picture of a house. He felt very happy.

He said, "Becky, were you ever engaged?"

"What does that mean?"

"Did you ever promise to marry any boy?"

"No."

"Would you like to be engaged?"

"What do you do?"

"You tell a boy that you will marry him. Then you kiss. That is all. It is easy."

"Why do you kiss?"

"They always do that. Do you remember what I was writing?"

"Yes."

"What was it? Shall I tell you?"

"Yes—but not now. Tomorrow."

"No. Now." He put his arm around her and said the words quietly. "Now you tell me."

She made him turn his face away as she said, "I—love—you!"

Tom kissed her and said, "Now it is all finished, Becky. And always after this you can only love me and can only marry me."

"And you can't marry any girl but me."

"Of course. That is part of it. And we will walk to school together. Because we are engaged."

"It is nice. I never heard of it before."

"Oh, it is good. Me and Amy Lawrence—"

Her big eyes told him that he had said the wrong thing.

"Oh, Tom! I am not the first girl that you were engaged to!" She began to cry.

"I do not love her now. I only love you."

More crying.

Tom took his favorite thing from his pocket. It was a gold-colored ball.

"Becky, take this."

She hit it from his hand to the floor.

Tom was angry and walked out of the school, and into the hills. He did not return.

Becky had not really wanted him to go, and when he did not return, she called, "Tom! Come back!" and cried again.

8
Tom Decides What to Do

Half an hour later Tom was sitting under a tree in the forest. He was very sad. He wished he could die—for a short time.

But soon he began to think of living again. He would travel to many countries. How would Becky feel then? He would become famous. Or he would join the Indians. But no, there was something better. He would be a pirate and steal gold from other ships. Tom Sawyer the Pirate!

Yes, it was decided. He would start the next morning.

Suddenly he heard a call from far away in the forest.

Now he was not Tom Sawyer. He was Robin Hood.

Moving slowly he called, "Stay where you are. Do not move until I call."

He saw Joe Harper. Tom called, "Stop! Who comes here into Sherwood Forest? No person enters my forest until I say that he may!"

"I am Guy of Guisborne," said Joe Harper, continuing the game. "I go where I want. Who are you?"

"I am Robin Hood. Soon you will be dead."

"Are you really that famous man? I am happy to fight you."

They began a slow and careful fight. Then Tom said, "Now fight faster."

Soon they were tired. "Fall!" Tom said. "You must fall!"

"You fall! I am fighting better than you." "But the story of Robin Hood says that I kill you. Turn and let me hit you in the back."

Joe turned, was hit and fell.

"Now," Joe said, rising, "You must let me kill you."

"I can't do that. It is not in the story."

"It should be."

"OK, Joe, you can be Robin, and you can kill me."

Joe agreed, and more fighting followed.

When the boys went home, they were sad because Robin Hood had lived so long ago. They would have liked living with him in Sherwood Forest better than being President of the United States.

9
Indian Joe Explains

At nine that night Tom and Sid were sent to bed as always. They prayed, and Sid quickly went to sleep. Tom was waiting.

Time passed very slowly and soon Tom was asleep. In his dreams he heard a cat call. Then a neighbor opened a window. Tom heard this, and quickly jumped out of his window making a sound like a cat. Huckleberry Finn was there with his dead cat.

In half an hour the boys were in the graveyard.

It was on a hill near the village. Tom was afraid that the sound of the wind came from the spirits of the dead. The boys found the new grave and sat down under a tree near it.

"Huck, do you believe that the dead people are

pleased to have us here?"

"I wish I knew."

"Huck, do you think Williams hears us talking?"

"His spirit hears us."

Tom touched Huck's arm. "Did you hear it? There it is again! Now you hear it."

The two boys were afraid and held each other close.

"Tom, they are coming! What shall we do?"

"I don't know. Will they see us?"

"Tom, they can see in the dark, like cats. I wish I had not come."

"Oh, don't be afraid. We are doing nothing. If we are quiet, they won't see us."

"I will try, Tom. But I am afraid."

"Listen!"

The sound of voices got closer.

"Look! See there!" said Tom. "What is it?"

"They are devils. Oh, Tom, this is very bad."

Some voices came very near, carrying a light. The boys were very afraid. "It is the devils. Three of them. We are in great trouble Tom. Can you pray?"

"I will try." Tom began to pray.

"Tom! They are human! That is old Muff Potter's voice. He is drunk, as always. He won't see us."

"Huck, I know another voice. It is Indian Joe."

"Why are they here?"

Then the boys were quiet because the three men had arrived at the new grave. "Here it is," said the third voice. The boys saw the face of young Doctor Robinson.

"Be quick," he said.

The other two men began opening the grave. It was very quiet. They opened the box and took out the body. Potter had a knife. "Now, Doctor, it is ready. But you must give us five dollars more."

"You have your money," the doctor said.

"No, you must give us more," Indian Joe said.

The doctor hit him suddenly, and Indian Joe fell.

Potter dropped his knife. "You hit my friend," he said and began fighting with the doctor.

Indian Joe stood up and picked up Potter's knife. He waited for a chance to stab the doctor. Suddenly the doctor hit Potter, who fell to the ground.

Indian Joe saw his chance and stabbed the doctor. The doctor fell to the ground. And the two boys ran away.

Slowly the doctor died. Indian Joe put the knife in Potter's right hand and then waited for him to wake up.

Soon Potter began to move. He saw the knife in his hand. Then he saw the doctor's body. "What happened, Joe?" he said.

"It is bad," said Joe. "Why did you do it?"

"I didn't do it!" Potter was afraid. "I was drunk. I don't remember. Did I do it, Joe? I never wanted to do it."

"He hit you and then you did it. But you are a good friend, Muff Potter. I won't tell anyone."

"Oh, Joe, thank you." And Potter began to cry.

"There is no time to cry. We must leave quickly. Move, now."

Potter started running. Joe watched him. "He forgot his knife because he is drunk. When he remembers, he will be afraid to return for it." Joe left.

The dead doctor, the body and the opened box were alone in the graveyard.

10
The Promise—The Boys are Afraid

The two boys were very afraid. They ran to the village and into an old, empty building.

"Huckleberry, what will happen now?"

"If the doctor dies, they will hang Indian Joe."

Tom spoke. "But who will tell about it? You and I?"

"If we tell and Indian Joe does not die, he will

kill us. Maybe Muff Potter will tell what happened. He is usually drunk."

Tom said, "Muff Potter does not know what happened. The doctor hit him. Huck, are you sure that you won't tell?"

"Tom, we can't tell. Indian Joe would kill us like two cats if we told. Tom, we must never tell. We must make a promise. In writing."

Tom agreed. On a piece of wood he wrote:

Huck Finn and Tom Sawyer promise they will never tell about this, and they wish they may die if they ever tell.

Then each boy cut a finger and signed in blood, TS and HF. Tom helped Huck to write his H and F.

Then they put the piece of wood in the ground.

Tom entered his house through his bedroom window. It was almost morning. He went to bed quietly, thinking that his aunt would never know. But Sid was not sleeping.

The next morning his aunt gave him some food. Then she cried, and asked why he couldn't be good. She wanted him to be good, but she couldn't help any more.

Tom also cried and promised to be good. But he felt that she did not believe him.

He went to school, where the teacher hit him and Joe Harper because they had run away from school the day before.

Then he went to his seat. On his chair was the bright, gold-like ball that he had given to Becky Thatcher. Now his heart was broken.

11
Tom is Worried

Soon everyone knew the bad news about the doctor and the teacher closed the school.

Potter's knife had been found. Someone saw Potter washing in a small river, in the early morning. This was strange because Potter never washed.

All the people in the town were slowly going toward the graveyard. Tom and Huckleberry went too, but they did not want to go. Tom was afraid when he saw the grave again and very afraid when he saw Indian Joe.

Then Muff Potter went to the grave. Some people saw him and shouted. He was with a policeman. Potter looked afraid when he saw the dead doctor and began to cry.

"I did not do it, friends," he said. "I did not do it."

"Who said that you did?" a voice shouted.

Potter saw Indian Joe, and said:

"Oh, Indian Joe, you promised me that you would never—"

"Is this your knife?" the policeman asked.

Potter fell to the ground.

"Tell them, Joe. Tell them."

Indian Joe told his story.

Huckleberry and Tom stood still and were not able to speak.

They wished to tell the true story, but were too afraid.

For a week Tom could not sleep well. One morning Sid said, "Tom, you talk in your sleep so much that I can't sleep."

Tom's face became white and he looked away. "This is bad," said Aunt Polly. "What is wrong, Tom?"

"Nothing," he answered.

"And you say bad things!" Sid said. "Last night you said, 'He's dead! He's dead!' Then you said,

'Do not hurt me. I will not tell!' Tell what?"

Aunt Polly said, "I understand. It is about the doctor. I dream about it too."

Mary said that she also dreamed about it, and then Sid stopped talking.

Slowly Tom could sleep easier.

Almost every day, Tom went to the prison window and gave Potter some small present. Then he felt happier.

The village people wanted to put Indian Joe in prison too. Like Muff Potter, he had been helping the doctor to carry away the dead body from the grave. But the people did nothing. Everyone was afraid of Indian Joe.

cry. He went faster and faster around the room. Aunt Polly arrived as Peter jumped through the open window with a cry.

Tom was laughing a lot.

"Tom, what is wrong with the cat?"

"Cats always do that to show they are happy."

But Aunt Polly saw the Painkiller. She knew what had happened. She caught Tom's ear and pulled him up, then hit him with her hand. "Why did you do that to the cat?"

"Because I am sorry that he has no aunt to care for him."

"Has no aunt! Why do you say that?"

"Because if he had an aunt she would give him a drink that burned his mouth and not think of his feelings. She would say, if the drink was good for a human, it would be good for a cat."

Aunt Polly thought. If it hurt a cat, it would hurt a boy, also. She put her hand on Tom's head. "I was trying to help you."

"And I was trying to help Peter. And it helped

him. I never saw him move so fast." He was smiling at her now.

"Oh, Tom! I will not give you any more Painkiller. Go to school. And try to be a good boy."

Tom arrived early at school and waited at the gate. He did not play. He said he was sick.

Jeff Thatcher came down the road, and Tom's face was brighter. But quickly it was dark again. Jeff was alone.

When Tom saw a girl's dress from far away, he watched and watched. But the girl was never the right one.

Then one more dress came through the gate. Tom's heart jumped. Soon, he was outside again, shouting, laughing, running, standing on his head to make Becky Thatcher watch him.

She never looked at him. How could she not see him? He ran through a group of boys, and he fell at her feet.

She turned away with her nose in the air. "Some people always want other people to look at them!"

His face became red. He stood straight and walked quietly away.

13
The Young Pirates

Tom had decided. He was a sad boy with no friends. No one loved him. He had tried to be good, but they would not let him. They were making him bad.

Far from the village he met his best friend, Joe Harper. Tom said that he was going to travel around the world, never to return to the village, and Joe wanted to go with him.

Joe's mother had hit him, even when he had done nothing. She must want him to go away, so he was going. He hoped she would be happy now and

would never be sorry about sending her boy into the cold world to die.

The two boys walked together. They agreed to be like brothers until they died. They began to plan. They decided to be pirates.

They decided the island in the Mississippi River, near the village, would be a good place. The island was long, with many trees. No people lived on it.

They met Huckleberry Finn, and he joined them.

Each boy would find food and other useful things. Then they would meet at night by the river.

Tom arrived with meat and a few other things. He called two times. Then a voice said:

"Who goes there?"

"Tom Sawyer the Black Pirate. Name your names."

"Huck Finn the Red-Handed and Joe Harper the Destroyer of the Seas." Tom had taken these names from his favorite books.

"Speak the word."

Two voices spoke together: "Blood!"

Tom joined them.

Joe Seas had also brought meat, and Finn had cigarettes. The Black Pirate said that they must also have fire. They went to a large river-boat.

The boat-men were all in the village. Next to the river-boat was a raft. They took it and moved down the river.

After two hours their raft touched the island. They would sleep in the open air.

They built a fire and cooked some meat. It was wonderful to be eating in the forest, far from other people. They said that they would never return to a village again.

After eating, they sat on the ground. Huck smoked a cigarette.

Huck said, "What do pirates do?"

Tom said, "Oh, they enjoy life. They follow other ships and catch them and burn them. They take the money from those ships and put it in a deep hole in the ground on their island. And they kill the people on the ships."

"They carry the women to the island," said Joe. "They don't kill the women."

"No," Tom agreed. "Pirates are good. They don't kill the women. And the women are always beautiful."

"And their clothes are gold," said Joe.

"Whose clothes?" said Huck.

"The pirates'."

Huck looked at his clothes. "Then I am not dressed right," he said. "But these are my only clothes."

The other boys told him that the fine clothes would come later.

Slowly their talk ended. Huck went to sleep quickly. But the other boys could not sleep so quickly. They began to think. Had it been wrong to run away from home? Had it been wrong to take the meat? They decided that they would never take meat or other people's things again.

And with that decided, they also went to sleep.

14
Island Life—Tom Quietly Leaves

Opening his eyes, Tom forgot where he was. Then he remembered.

The forest was very quiet. Joe and Huck were still sleeping.

The life of the forest began to wake up. Birds started singing. Small animals moved in the trees.

Tom called to the others. Soon they were all playing in the river. Their raft had been carried away, but this pleased them. Now they were sure that they would never return to their village.

Happy and hungry, they built their fire. Huck had found some good water to drink. Joe cooked some meat. Tom and Huck went to the river to catch fish. The fish was very good. After that, they walked through the trees. The island was long and narrow. It was very near one river-bank, but far from the bank where the village was.

They played in the river often. In the afternoon they returned to their fire. They ate some meat again and talked.

But the talk soon stopped. They began to feel sad. Tom and Joe were thinking of home. Huck, who had no home, was thinking of the places where he usually went to sleep.

But they did not tell each other they felt sad.

Suddenly, they heard a sound. They looked at each other, and listened. Quiet—Bang! Then quiet, and then again, Bang!

"We must go and see."

They ran to the river near the town and looked across the water.

They saw a big river-boat. It was coming slowly down the river. There were many people on it. There were many small boats around it.

"I understand!" said Tom. "Someone has died in the river!"

"That is right," said Huck. "They did that last summer when Bill Turner died in the river. They look for the body when it rises to the top of the water."

"I wish that I was on that river-boat now," said Joe.

"Who do you think has died?" said Huck.

They listened and watched. Suddenly Tom said "Boys, I know! They are looking for us!"

This was a wonderful thing to know. Everyone was looking for them. People were sorry that they had not always been kind to them. The town was talking about them. This was fine.

It was good to be a pirate.

That evening they ate more fish. Then they talked about what the village people were thinking and saying. Slowly they stopped talking and sat looking into the fire. Tom and Joe thought of people at home who may be sad. Joe began to speak of returning to the village.

Tom and Huck laughed at him.

Huck went to sleep. Then Joe went to sleep. Tom sat for a long time.

Then he stood up. He found two pieces of wood on which he could write. After writing on the wood, he put one piece in Joe's hat. He put the other in his pocket.

Then he ran quietly toward the river.

15
Tom Learns What is Happening

A few minutes later Tom was walking through the water toward the bank. He sat in the small boat tied next to the river-boat. The river-boat began to move. He knew that this was the last time it would cross the river that night. Twelve minutes later the boat stopped. Tom got out and ran to the village.

Soon he was outside his aunt's house. He looked through a window into a room. There sat Aunt Polly, Sid, Mary, and Joe Harper's mother. They were talking. They were next to the bed, and the bed was between them and the door.

Tom went to the door and opened it quietly. He moved quickly across the room and under the bed. No one saw him.

"But," said Aunt Polly, "he was not bad. He was

only full of life, like any young animal. He did not want to do bad things. And he was a very kind boy." She began to cry.

"My Joe was the same. He was not really bad. And he was always kind. And now I shall never see him again!"

"I am sorry now for so many things! Only yesterday, the cat—" Crying, Aunt Polly told about the cat and the Painkiller. Tom was crying a little now. He could hear Mary crying too. Had he really always been a good boy? It was surprising. But now he was beginning to believe it. He wished to run to his aunt and make her happy. But he waited and listened.

Their raft had been found on the river. There was no hope. On Sunday everyone in the village would go to the church and pray for the boys.

Mrs. Harper went home. Sid and Mary went to bed. Then Aunt Polly prayed for Tom. Her words and her old voice were filled with love. Tom began to cry again.

Then she got into bed. It was a long time before she went to sleep.

Tom came out and looked at her. He loved her and he was very sorry for her. He took the piece of wood with his writing on it out of his pocket. He put it on a table. She would see it there in the morning.

But then a new thought came to him. He put the wood into his pocket again. Then he gave his aunt a kiss and left the house.

He ran to the river. He took a small boat and went back to the island.

Soon he was on the island. He heard Joe say:

"No. Tom is true, Huck. He will return. What do you think he has been doing?"

"Here I am!" cried Tom, stepping out from among the trees.

They ate fish while Tom told what he had been doing. Then Tom went to sleep until noon.

16
A Night Surprise

The boys played in the water. But the next day Joe was very sad. Would he ever be happy again? Huck also was sad. Tom was not happy, but he tried to look happy. He had something interesting to tell them, but he did not want to tell them yet.

He said, trying to look happy, "I think there have been pirates on this island before. Maybe they left an old box full of money? Shall we go and look for it."

But the other boys were not interested.

Joe said, "I want to go home. I am very sad here."

"Oh, no, Joe. You will feel better soon," said Tom. "Think of the good fishing here."

"I am not interested in fishing. I want to go home."

"But, Joe, this is the best swimming place."

"I don't want to swim. I want to go home."

"Baby! You want to see your mother."

"Yes, I do want to see my mother. And you would want to see your mother if you had a mother. I am not a baby."

"But you like it here, Huck? You want to stay? You and I will stay?"

Huck said, "Y-e-s." He was not sure.

"Let Joe go, if he wants to go," Tom said.

"We do not need him."

Joe began to walk into the water to swim toward the village.

Tom looked at Huck. Huck looked away. Then Huck said, "I want to go, Tom. We can go, Tom, can't we?"

"I won't! You can go. But I am going to stay."

Huck started to walk sadly away. Tom wanted to follow. He hoped that they would stop, but they didn't. Suddenly Tom felt very sad and quiet.

He ran after the other boys, shouting, "Wait!

Wait! I want to tell you something."

They stopped, and he ran toward them. They listened to him without an answering word or smile. As they began to understand they became happy and shouted.

That night, after eating, Tom wanted to learn to smoke. Joe wanted to try too. With Huck's help, they began.

Tom said, "This is easy. I could have learned long ago."

"This is nothing," said Joe. "I could do this all day. I don't feel sick."

Tom said, "I wish that the other boys could see us now. We won't tell them. And some time when they are with us, I will say, 'Joe, I want to smoke.' And you will say, 'My cigarettes are not very good.' And I will say, 'It does not need to be good if it is strong.'

"That will be good, Tom! I wish we could do it now!"

"And we will tell them that we learned to smoke

when we were pirates. And they will wish that they had been here!"

The talk continued for a short time, then stopped. Joe said, "I am going for a walk."

Tom said, "Let me go with you."

Huck sat down again and waited an hour. Then he was sad, and went to find his friends. Both were sleeping.

That night they did not talk much. When Huck began to smoke, they said no. Something they had eaten made them feel sick.

That night Joe opened his eyes and called to the other boys. The air was strange and heavy and hot. They were afraid. They sat together and waited.

A light filled the sky. Bright light. A loud sound. A cold wind. The light came and went away again, and the sound that followed became louder and louder. There was a strong wind and rain began to fall.

"Quick, boys, find a safe place," Tom shouted.

They ran to different places. Then heavy rain

came down and they thought the island would be washed away.

But then the storm grew weaker and weaker and it became quiet again.

The boys saved their fire and cooked some meat on it.

In the morning, they all wanted to go home. Tom tried to find a new game to interest them.

He found one. Now they were Indians. Fighting Indians. But when the day ended, they smoked together, as Indians always did to show they were at peace. And two of them were happy it did not make them sick.

17
Tom's Plan Succeeds

But no-one was happy in the village that same afternoon. The village was quiet. Nobody spoke and children stopped playing.

Becky Thatcher was walking near the school. She thought, "Oh, I wish I had not returned the bright ball Tom gave me! I have nothing to help me remember him. He is gone now, and I shall never, never see him again."

She walked away crying.

A large group of boys and girls, friends of Tom's and Joe's, came to the school to look at the yard where they had played together. They spoke of things Tom and Joe had said and done. They tried to learn who was the last person to see the two boys. The children who were the last to talk with

Tom and Joe felt very important.

One boy who also wanted to feel important said, "I had a fight with Tom Sawyer, and he was stronger than me."

But most of the boys could say that.

The next morning everyone in the village went to the church. Outside the church they talked, but in the church they were very quiet.

The little church was full. Aunt Polly entered, followed by Sid and Mary and the Harper family. All were wearing black clothes. The other people in the church stood up, while the two families walked to the front of the church and sat down.

It was quiet again. They all prayed, and then sang a song. Now the church leader began to talk about the boys and how good they had been. People were sorry that they had thought these boys were bad. Everyone was crying.

Slowly the church door opened. One by one, everyone turned to look. Then everyone turned to look while the three dead boys walked to the front

of the church. Tom was first, Joe next, and last came Huck. They had been listening to every word!

Aunt Polly, Mary, and the Harpers put their arms around Tom and Joe. Huck stood alone, not knowing what to do. He started to move away, but Tom stopped him and said:

"Aunt Polly, this is not right. Some person must be glad to see Huck."

"And some person shall be me. I am glad to see him, dear boy!" She put her arms around Huck too. And now Huck felt stranger than before.

"Sing! And sing your best!" cried the church leader.

Everyone was happy and sang loudly. It was the best church singing ever! Tom Sawyer knew that this was the best time in his life.

18

Tom's Wonderful Dream

That was Tom's great plan—to return home with the other boys and go to the church to hear people praying for them. They had crossed the river at night and sat in the forest until morning. They went to sleep in the church until the people came. Then they appeared at the most important time.

The next morning, Aunt Polly and Mary were very loving to Tom. He had everything that he wanted to eat. They talked a lot. Aunt Polly said:

"We can laugh now, Tom. But you were not kind to let me worry. You came across the river to surprise us in the church. Why could you not come across the river to tell me that you were not dead?"

"Yes, you could have done that, Tom," said Mary.

"Would you, Tom?" said Aunt Polly. "If you had

thought of it, would you have come to tell me?"

"Tom is always in a hurry," Mary said. "He never thinks."

"Sid would have thought. And Sid would have come. Tom, one day you will be sorry. You will wish that you had cared more for me. But then it will be too late."

"I do care for you," said Tom. "I wish that I had thought. But I dreamed about you."

"A cat does that. What did you dream?"

"I dreamed that I saw you sitting there by the bed. Sid and Mary were sitting with you. And I dreamed that Joe Harper's mother was here."

"She was, one night. Did you dream any more?"

"Yes. But I can't remember all of it."

"Try, Tom. Try to remember."

"You said that the door must be open because you could feel the wind coming in. You said that was strange. And you told Sid—"

"What did I tell Sid, Tom?"

"You told him—oh, you told him to close the

door. And you were talking about me. I remember better now. You said that I was not bad. You said that I was only wild and full of life like a—like any young animal."

"I am surprised! And some people say that dreams are never true. Tell me more, Tom."

"And then you began to cry."

"Yes, I did. I did."

"Then Mrs. Harper began to cry. She said that Joe was good also. And then you told about me giving the Painkiller to the cat. And then everyone talked about finding our bodies, and praying in church on Sunday."

"It is all true!"

"And Mrs. Harper went home. And you prayed for me—and I could see you and hear every word. You went to bed, and I was very sorry for you. And I had a letter for you. It was on a piece of wood. On the wood were the words, 'We are not dead—we are away being pirates.' I gave you a kiss and went away again."

"Did you, Tom? Did you?" She gave him a big hug.

"It was very kind, but it was only a dream," said Sid.

"Be quiet, Sid! And Tom, here is a big apple for you. And now, children, go to school."

Tom walked slowly, feeling that everyone was watching him. Smaller boys followed him, happy to be seen with him. Boys his own age wished they had sun-tanned skin and were famous like him.

Tom decided that he was no longer interested in Becky Thatcher. He was happy being famous. When Becky arrived at school, Tom pretended not to see her. But he saw her playing with other boys and girls. And she often came near to him and looked at him.

And he began talking to Amy Lawrence.

Becky tried to go away from him, but her feet would not move. They carried her near to the group around Tom. She said to one of the girls, "Mary, where were you yesterday? I wanted to tell you about the picnic."

"Oh, who's picnic?"

"My mother is going to let me have one."

"I hope that she will let me come."

"I may ask anyone I want. I want you and all my friends to come." She looked at Tom, but he was talking to Amy Lawrence. Others in the group began asking if they could go. Soon everyone had asked. Only Tom and Amy had not asked. Tom turned away.

Becky was sad and wanted to cry. She went away alone to think what to do.

When Tom saw her again, she and a boy called Alfred Temple were sitting together looking at a book. Now Tom suddenly wanted to stop talking to Amy. He left her and went to look again at Becky and Alfred. Becky pretended not to see Tom. But she saw him, and she was happy.

"That Alfred Temple!" Tom thought. "And his fine clothes! I will catch him! And I will—"

He began hitting the air as if he were fighting with the other boy.

At noon Tom went home. Becky again looked at the book with Alfred, hoping that Tom would see them. But Tom did not.

Suddenly she began to cry. She left Alfred and walked away.

Alfred followed, hoping to find some way to make her happy again. But she said:

"Go away! I never want to see you again!"

Alfred was quick to understand. Becky had been trying to make Tom unhappy. He felt angry and went into the school. He saw one of Tom's books and thought how he could hurt Tom. He opened the book to the page they were going to study that afternoon. He tore the page so it looked like Tom had done it.

Becky, looking in the window, saw him do it. She thought of telling Tom. Then she decided that she would not. She would let the teacher hit Tom for tearing his book.

19

Tom Tells the Truth

Tom arrived home feeling very sad. His aunt's first words made him feel more sad.

"Tom, I want to hit you!"

"Aunt Polly, what have I done?"

"I went to see Mrs. Harper to tell her about your dream. Joe had already told her that you were here that night. I believed your story was a dream. Why did you say it was a dream?"

"Aunt Polly, I wish I had not done it. I did not think."

"Oh, child, you never think. You never think of anything but yourself. "

"Aunt Polly, I know that it was bad. But I did not plan to be bad. And I did not come here that night to laugh at you. I came to tell you that we were not dead. I did not want you to be sad."

"Tom, I would like to believe that. But I don't think that you had such a thought."

"Yes, I did, I did. It is true. I wanted to save you from being sad."

"Then why did you not tell me, child?"

"You began talking of Sunday and all the people praying for us in the church. And I began thinking about going there on Sunday. And I put my letter in my pocket and went away."

"What letter?"

"The letter to tell you that we were pirates. I wish now that you had opened your eyes when I gave you a kiss."

"Did you kiss me, Tom? Are you sure?"

"Yes, I did, Aunt."

"Why?"

"Because I loved you and you were crying in your sleep and I was sorry."

The words sounded true. The old lady said, "Kiss me again, Tom! And then go to school."

When he was gone, she looked at his little coat. In the pocket she found a piece of wood with writing on it. She read the words and tears fell from her eyes. Then she said, "Now I can forget anything bad that boy does. I could forget a million bad things."

20
Becky Has a Problem

Tom was happy again. He started walking to school, and saw Becky Thatcher, also going to school. He ran to her and said:

"I am sorry I was bad this morning, Becky. I won't ever be like that again. Please let us be friends."

The girl stopped and looked into his face. "Go away, Mr. Thomas Sawyer. I will never speak to you again."

Then she started walking again. Tom was so surprised he could not think of anything to say. He was angry. If she were a boy, he would fight her.

Becky was also angry. Soon the teacher would hit Tom for tearing his book.

She did not know that she would soon have trouble too!

The teacher had a book that he was studying. Every day he would read some pages when he was not busy. Every boy and girl in the school knew about this book, but no-one had ever seen it. Now, as Becky passed the teacher's table, she saw the book. She opened it and began to look at it.

Suddenly Tom opened the door. Becky quickly closed the book. But her hand caught the page, and suddenly, it was in two pieces. Becky began to cry.

"You are bad, Tom Sawyer, to come and watch me! And now you will tell the teacher, and he will hit me. What should I do? I have never been hit in school. But I know what is going to happen to you. You wait and see!" Then she ran outside crying.

Tom said to himself: "How silly that girl is! Being hit in school is nothing. And I will not tell who opened the book. The teacher will ask who did it. He will call each name. And when he says the right one, he won't need an answer. He will see the answer in her face."

School began, and soon Tom's book was discovered. He said that he had not torn the page, but the teacher did not believe him. The teacher hit Tom, and Becky watched, trying to feel happy about this. But she almost stood up to say it was Alfred Temple.

One hour later, the boys and girls were busy with their books. The teacher opened his book. Tom looked at Becky. He wished that he could help her, but what could he do?

The teacher stood before the school. Everyone was afraid of him.

"Who did this to my book?"

No one spoke.

"Benjamin Rogers?"

"No."

"Joe Harper?"

"No."

"Amy Lawrence?"

"No."

"Gracie Miller?"

"No."

The next name was Becky Thatcher. Tom was afraid, but he saw that she was more afraid.

"Becky Thatcher, look at me! Did you do this to my book?"

Tom jumped to his feet and shouted, "I did it." Everyone looked at him. They could not believe what they had heard.

Tom stood up to be hit. But the look of surprise, thanks and love in Becky's eyes was enough for being hit a hundred times.

21
ff's Friends

...ner holidays.

...o long. Tom did not have

...e a diary of everything that
...g happened for three days. He
...was no good.

...s living in another town with
...other during the summer.

...ered the killing in the grave-
...k.

...m stayed in bed. He was very
...ed in nothing. Then he was
...ay he was ill again. He was in
...weeks.

...iet village something began to

happen. A judge was coming to listen to the story of the killing in the graveyard. He would decide what to do about Muff Potter.

Every person in the village talked of this. And Tom felt afraid. He took Huck to a quiet place. He wanted to be sure that Huck had not told the story.

"Huck, have you told about—that?"

"Oh. No, I have not."

"Never a word?"

"Never a word. Why do you ask?"

"I was afraid."

"Tom Sawyer, we would not live two days if that story was told. You know that."

"Huck, could any person make you tell?"

"If I wanted Indian Joe to kill me, they could make me tell."

"Good! I think that we are safe if we do not talk."

"What talk have you heard, Huck?"

"Talk? It is all Muff Potter, Muff Potter, Muff Potter."

"I hear the same talk. They are going to hang him. Do you feel sorry for him sometimes?"

"Almost always—almost always. He has never done anything to hurt another person. He only fishes to get some money so that he can get drunk. He is really good. Once he gave me a fish, when he really did not have enough for himself. And he helped me at other times when I needed help."

"He helped me, also, Huck. He helped me to catch fish. I wish that I could get him out of jail."

"We can't get him out, Tom. And if we did, they would catch him again."

"Yes…but he did not do it."

The boys talked for a long time, but it did not make them happy. As night came, they went to the jail. They went to the window and gave Potter some cigarettes. They had done this before.

He was always very happy to get their presents, and his thanks always hurt them. It hurt them even more when Potter said:

"You have been good to me, boys. Better than

the others in this town. And I won't forget, I won't. Often I say to myself, 'I was good to all the boys. I showed them where the good fishing was. I was their friend when I could be a friend. And now they forget old Muff when he has trouble. But Tom does not forget, and Huck does not—they do not forget him,' I say, 'and I won't forget them.'

"But, boys, I did a bad thing. I was drunk. Now I must die for it. But we won't talk about that. I won't make you feel sad. You have been my friends.

"But I want to say this. Never get drunk. Then you won't ever be where I am now.

"You are the only ones who come here. Let me touch your hands. Little hands, and weak, but they have helped Muff Potter. And they would help him more if they could."

Tom went home feeling very, very sad. During the next two days he went to the town meeting house. The judge was listening to the story of the killing. Tom wanted to go inside, but stayed out-side.

Huck was having the same experience.

They were careful not to meet each other. Tom listened when people came out. The news was always bad. At the end of the second day people said that Indian Joe's story never changed. Everyone knew what the judge would decide.

All the people in the village went to the meeting house the next morning. This was to be the important day. There was no hope for Potter. The judge arrived. And Indian Joe was there, too.

A man was asked about the killing. He said he saw Muff Potter washing his hands in the river. It was the morning after the killing.

Another man was asked to tell his story. He told about finding the knife near the doctor's body.

Another man spoke about the knife. He knew that it was Potter's knife.

A man who had studied law sat next to Muff Potter. He was there to help Potter. But he asked no questions as these men told their stories. It was strange.

More men told their stories. And the man next to Potter asked them no questions.

After a while, all the stories against Potter had been told. Then the man next to Potter stood up. He spoke to the judge:

"Sir, we planned to show that Muff Potter was drunk that night. We planned to show that he did not know what he was doing. But we have changed our plans. We wish to ask Thomas Sawyer some questions."

Everyone was surprised. Potter was very surprised. Every eye was watching Tom. He stood up and walked to the front of the meeting house. He was afraid.

The questions began.

"Thomas Sawyer, where were you on the night of the killing?"

Tom looked at Indian Joe, and he could not speak. But then he felt stronger and said:

"In the graveyard!"

"Louder, please. Do not be afraid. You were—"

"In the graveyard."

He looked at Indian Joe's face. He saw a cold smile. Then it was gone.

"Were you near Hoss Williams's grave?"

"Yes."

"Louder, please. How near were you?"

"As near as I am to you."

"Could you be seen?"

"No. I was in the trees near the grave."

"Was another person with you?"

"Yes. I went there with—"

"That is enough. We will call him when we need him. Did you carry something there?"

Tom did not answer.

"Speak, my boy. What did you carry there?"

"Only a—a—dead cat."

Some people laughed.

"We plan to show the bones of that cat. Now, my boy, tell us everything that happened—tell it as you wish, but tell it all and do not be afraid."

Tom began slowly. Everyone looked at him.

Interest in his story became greater and greater.

"—and as the doctor hit Muff Potter and Muff Potter fell, Indian Joe jumped with the knife and—"

Indian Joe jumped through a window, and was gone.

22
Happy Days and Bad Nights

Tom was famous again. The old people loved him and the young people wished they were like him. His name was in the village newspaper.

Everyone was kind to Muff Potter. Tom's days were happy, but at night he dreamed of Indian Joe.

Poor Huck felt the same. Huck had not been called in the meeting-house but he was afraid. Huck did not trust anyone, because Tom had broken their promise.

Every day, Muff Potter's thanks made Tom glad that he had told his story. Every night he wished that he had not opened his mouth.

Sometimes Tom was afraid that Indian Joe would never be caught. He felt he could never be safe until Indian Joe was dead.

Indian Joe had not been found.

The days passed and Tom did not feel so afraid.

23
Hunt for Gold

There comes a time in every boy's life when he wants to hunt for gold that pirates have put deep in the earth.

Tom met Huck Finn who agreed to do anything that would take time but not money.

"Where can we find gold?" said Huck.

"Oh, only in very special places. Sometimes on islands, sometimes in old boxes under an old, dead tree, but usually under the floor in an old house."

"Who puts it there?"

"People who take it away from other people."

"Why do they put it in the ground? If I were rich, I would spend my money and enjoy it."

"I would too. But these people are different."

"Why don't they return and get it?"

"They think they will, but they forget where it is. Or they die."

"How are you going to find it, Tom? Where will you look?"

"We tried looking for gold on the island when we were pirates. I know where there is a very old house. And there are old, dead trees everywhere."

"How do you know which tree to choose?"

"Choose all of them!"

"Tom, we shall be working all summer!"

"What is wrong with that? We could find a hundred dollars. Or gold. How would you like that?"

Huck looked excited. "Give me the hundred dollars, and you can have the gold."

The boys got some gardening things. Then they walked to an old, dead tree outside the village. They were very hot and sat down to rest.

Tom said, "Huck, if we find some money, what will you do with it?"

"Spend it! Before my father takes it and spends it. What will you do with yours?"

"I will marry."

"Marry! Tom, you would be mad. Think of my father and mother. They were fighting all the time."

"The girl I will marry won't fight."

"Tom, they are all the same. Who is she?"

"I won't tell you now."

"If you marry, I will be sadder than I am now."

"No, you won't. You will come to live with me. Now we must start working."

They worked for half an hour, but found no box of money. They worked for another half hour. Then Huck said:

"Is the money always so deep in the ground?"

"Not always. I don't think this is the right place."

They began again near another tree.

"Where shall we try next?" Huck said.

"There is an old tree on Cardiff Hill next to Mrs. Douglas's house."

"That might be a good place. But won't she take the money away from us? It is her land."

"If you find money in the ground, it's yours. It is not the land owners'."

They worked in the new place. After a while Tom said:

"We must be in the wrong place again. Maybe we should work at night."

The boys stopped work and returned to the tree that night. It was a very quiet place. They began to work.

They worked hard, but didn't find anything. Tom said: "Huck, we are wrong again."

"We should stop," Huck said. "I do not like the night. I am afraid."

"I feel the same, Huck. Can we try another place?"

"Where?"

"The old house."

"Tom, I am afraid of old houses. Let's go to the house during the day."

24
Sleeping Ghosts —
A Box Full of Gold

On Saturday afternoon the boys went to the old house. It was very quiet and they were afraid.

Quietly they went in. They did not speak. They looked around with interest.

They put their tools by the door.

Then they wanted to look at the room above.

They found nothing up there and started to go down when they heard a sound.

"We must run!"

"We can't. They are coming in."

The boys were on the floor, looking down into the room through holes. They were afraid.

Two men entered. Both boys knew one of them. He was very old. He had long white hair, and a white beard. The village people thought it sad that he could not hear and could not speak.

The other man was a stranger. He was wearing very old clothes. His face was not kind. He was talking as they entered.

The two men sat, with their backs against the wall.

"No," said the stranger. "I do not like it. They will catch us."

"You are mad!" said the man who everyone thought could not hear or speak. "You are afraid!"

Now the boys were very afraid. This man was Indian Joe!

Joe said, "We were not caught before."

"But that was different."

"They may catch us here in this house," Joe said. "I wanted to leave here yesterday. But those boys were playing on Cardiff Hill. They would have seen us."

"Those boys" were Tom and Huck. They were even more afraid. What would have happened to them yesterday, if they had come to this house? They wished that they had waited a year before coming.

The two men had brought some food, and they began to eat.

After a while Joe said, "When it is dark, go home. Wait there until you hear from me. And we will do the job we planned. And then we will run. Far away. Now I need sleep. You stay here and make sure it is safe."

He went to sleep. Soon the other man was sleeping too.

"Now is our chance—let's go!" said Tom.

Huck said. "I can't. I am too afraid."

Tom started to leave alone. But the old floor made lots of sounds, so he stopped.

The boys could not leave.

Slowly it became night.

Indian Joe woke up. He said, "It is time for us to go. What shall we do with our money? Shall we leave it here? Six hundred dollars is heavy to carry."

His friend agreed and took out a big bag of money.

The boys became interested. Six hundred dollars would make the boys rich! And they knew where Indian Joe was putting it.

Indian Joe found the boys' tools and used them to make a hole in the ground. The boys watched quietly. Now they were very glad they were there!

Then the tool hit something hard.

"Look!" Indian Joe said.

"What is it?" said his friend.

"It is an old box," Joe said. He opened it. "It's full of money!"

The men took the box out of the hole and looked at the money.

"There are thousands of dollars here," said Indian Joe.

"Now we don't need to do that job in the village," said the other.

Indian Joe said, "You do not understand. I am not doing that job only for money. Wrong was done to me, and I am going to get even. I need your help. Go home until I tell you to come."

"What shall we do with this money? Put it in the ground again?"

"Yes. (The boys were happy.) No! (The boys were sad.) Where did these tools come from? Who was here? Let's put the money at Number Two place, under the cross."

"It is dark. Let's go."

"Who do you think came here?" Indian Joe said. "Do you think they are still here?"

The boys' were afraid.

Indian Joe put his hand on his knife and started to go up the steps.

The boys could not move. They heard Joe coming.

Then they heard the steps breaking, and Indian Joe fell down.

"No one is here," his friend said. "They ran away when they saw us coming."

Soon the two men left the house with the box of

gold and the bag of dollars.

Tom and Huck watched them.

Now they were safe. They left the house and went back to the town.

In town, they decided to look for Indian Joe and find the Number Two place.

Tom had a bad thought. "Indian Joe said wrong was done to him and he was going to get even. Was he talking about us, Huck?"

Suddenly Huck was afraid too.

25
Bad Thoughts

Tom had bad dreams that night. Four times he had the gold in his hands. Four times he opened his eyes and had nothing. When he woke up everything was like a dream. The money was like a dream. He had never seen half a hundred dollars before. The day was like a dream. He decided to talk to Huck, but not to talk about the money. If it was a dream, Huck would not talk about it.

He found Huck fishing by the river. He looked very sad.

"Hello, Huck!"

"Hello, Tom."

No one said anything.

"Tom, if we had not put our tools by the door, we would have that money."

"It was not a dream, it was not a dream! But I almost wish that it was a dream."

"Dream! If Indian Joe had found us, you would know that it was not a dream!"

"We must find him! Find the money! We must find his Number Two place. It could be the number of a house."

"No, Tom. The houses in this town do not have numbers."

"It could be the number of a hotel room."

"Yes! There are only two hotels here."

"You stay here, Huck. I will go and find Number Two."

Tom went into town. A young man was staying in room Number Two at the first hotel.

Room Number Two was closed at the second hotel. But a light had been seen in the window the night before.

"That room is Indian Joe's Number Two, Huck."

"I think you are right, Tom. What shall we do?"

Tom thought.

"We must wait and try to go in at night. If you see Indian Joe you must follow him. If he doesn't go to the hotel, then it can't be his Number Two place."

"But I am too afraid to follow him alone, Tom!"

"It will be all right. He will not see you. If I see him, I will follow him."

26
Number Two—Huck Waits

They waited for three nights. The fourth night was very dark.

Huck stayed outside and Tom went into the hotel.

Huck waited. And waited. What had happened to Tom?

Suddenly Tom came running out of the hotel.

"Run! Run for your life!"

They ran out of town. It started to rain. They ran to an empty old building and went inside.

"Huck, I was really afraid! I opened the door and went into the room, and—Huck, I almost stepped on Indian Joe's hand!"

"No!"

"Yes! He was sleeping on the floor. Drunk, I think. I ran away."

"Tom, did you see the box?"

"No, I did not see the box. Only drink. The room is full of drink."

"Tom, if Joe is drunk, now is the time to get the money box."

"Is it? You get it."

Huck was afraid. "No, I don't think so."

"No, let's wait until Indian Joe leaves the room. Then we can go in fast and get the box. We must watch every night."

"I agree. Let me watch all night and every night. You do the other part of the job."

"Yes, you go and watch, Huck. And when you want me, come to my window and make a sound like a cat."

27
The Picnic — Indian Joe's Job

The next morning Tom heard the Thatcher family had returned. This was good news. For a while Tom forgot Indian Joe and the box of gold.

More good news. The next day there would be a picnic.

Everyone met at eleven in the morning and walked to the river. They would ride down the river on the old river-boat.

Sid was sick and did not go. Mary stayed with him.

Because it would finish late, Becky told her mother she would stay with Suzy Harper, who lived near the river.

They went down the river on the old river-boat and then stopped to eat and play by the big trees.

Then someone said, "Who wants to go into the cave?"

They took lights and entered.

Inside was very cold. The walls were rock with water running down them.

There were many rooms, big and small.

No one knew all the caves. They were too big.

But Tom Sawyer knew them best.

When they went outside it was night and people were calling them. It was time to go back to the town.

Huck saw the lights of the returning river-boat. He was already watching for Indian Joe. The night was very dark. It was eleven o'clock and everyone was sleeping.

Huck also wanted to sleep.

Suddenly he heard a sound. Then he saw two men. One was carrying something. It must be the box! Should he call Tom? No. The men would walk away with the box and it would never be found again. He would follow them.

Without shoes, Huck moved as quietly as a cat.

The men went out of the town and stopped by some trees near a house.

Mrs. Douglas lived alone in the house. Huck liked Mrs. Douglas, because she was kind to him. This must be the job Indian Joe and his friend had been talking about.

"Lets go in," said Indian Joe.

"Let's forget the job."

"No. You can have the money. I do not want it. But her husband put me in jail. Then he died. I can't hurt him. But she is still living. I can hurt her."

"You must not kill her!"

"I will not kill her. I am going to cut her face. For a woman this hurts more than being killed. You will help me or I will kill you. And then I will kill her too."

Huck knew he must get help. Quietly, he went down the hill. He ran to Mr. Jones's house and hit the door.

Mr. Jones and his two strong sons opened a window and looked out.

"Who are you? What do you want?"

"Huckleberry Finn. Quick, let me come in."

They let him in. "What do you want?"

"Please never tell that I told you," were Huck's first words. "I would be killed for sure—but Mrs. Douglas has been a good friend to me. I want to tell you."

"Speak," said the old man. "We will never tell, boy."

Three minutes later the old man and his sons, carrying guns, went up the hill to Mrs. Douglas's house.

Huck ran back to the town.

28
The Old Man Reports
—Everyone is Afraid

The next day was Sunday.

Early in the morning Huck went to the old man's house.

"Please let me come in! It is Huck Finn."

"That name will open this door night or day, boy!"

The boy was surprised. He had never heard these words before.

The old man opened the door. "Come in and have something to eat."

"What happened last night? I heard the guns and ran away. Are the men dead?"

"They are not dead, boy. We are sorry for that. They heard us coming, and they ran. Then we went

down to the village to get help. We will look for the two men today. I wish we had seen those two men. Could you see them in the dark?"

"Yes. One has long white hair. He can't hear and he can't talk." Then he told about the other man's face and clothes.

Mr. Jones asked Huck why he had followed the men up the hill.

Huck said that he thought one man was Indian Joe. But he did not tell about the box of money.

Soon people began coming to the house, and Huck went where they could not see him.

Mrs. Douglas came to thank Mr. Jones for helping her.

"You should not thank me," he said. "There is another person who did more to help you. But he does not want thanks."

Everyone went to church early that day. They wanted to talk about the two bad men who had not been found.

Leaving the church, Mrs. Thatcher walked with

Mrs. Harper. She said, "Is my Becky going to sleep all day?"

"Your Becky?"

"Yes. She stayed with you last night."

"No."

Mrs. Thatcher stopped suddenly. She looked ill. Then Aunt Polly joined them. She said, "Good morning, Mrs. Thatcher. Good morning, Mrs. Harper. Did my Tom stay with Joe last night without telling me?"

Mrs. Thatcher looked more ill than before. She moved her head, saying no.

"He did not stay with us," said Mrs. Harper. She was surprised.

Aunt Polly asked Joe Harper, "Have you seen my Tom this morning?"

"No."

"When did you last see him?"

But Joe could not remember.

Suddenly everyone started talking. No one could remember Tom or Becky returning on the river-boat

from the picnic. Someone said maybe they were lost in the caves.

Mrs. Thatcher and Aunt Polly began to cry. Everyone went to look for the children.

But the next morning they were still missing. Old Mr. Jones came home at noon and found that Huck was sick. Mrs. Douglas came to care for him.

The men looked in all parts of the cave. They shouted, but there was no answer. The strong men continued to look for three days and nights.

Huck asked about Tom Sawyer.

Mrs. Douglas said, "Quiet, child. You must not talk. You are very, very sick." She began to cry.

Everyone was afraid for Tom and Becky.

29
Lost, Then Found—But Not Saved

Tom and Becky had started walking with the other children. Then they had walked deeper and deeper into the caves. They found a small, beautiful river. Next to the river they found a new cave in the

rocks. They went in and as they walked it became darker and darker. And the children became more and more afraid and started to run.

Suddenly they came to a lake and it was very quiet.

Becky said "I want to go back. Do you know the way?"

"I think so," said Tom. But the more they walked, the more lost they became.

"Tom, we are lost!" Becky said. "We will never

find our way out. We will die here," she said and started to cry.

"I think I can find the way out. First we must return to the small river."

They walked and walked until they were too tired to walk any more.

"I'm very hungry," Becky said. Tom had saved some cake from the picnic. He took it out of his pocket and shared it with Becky.

Then they walked some more until they found the small, beautiful river.

Tom said. "I'm sorry, I still don't know the way back."

They were tired so they quickly went to sleep. They dreamed of home and food and day-light.

They didn't know how many days had passed. Maybe a week?

"I will look again for the way out," Tom said. He moved slowly. Suddenly he saw a hand holding a light.

Tom shouted.

At once a body followed the hand. It was Indian Joe!

Tom could not move because he was afraid. Indian Joe ran away.

He did not tell Becky what he had seen or why he had shouted.

He returned to the small river. They were both tired and hungry and afraid.

Tom promised Becky he would look after her. He held her hand as they went to sleep.

But he was afraid they would not find the way out.

30
Tom Tells the Story
of Their Escape

Sunday and two more days had passed. A few men continued to look for the children. Most of the people thought that they would never be found.

Mrs. Thatcher was very ill. Aunt Polly's hair had changed from gray to white.

Then, one night everyone in the village began to shout.

"They are found! The children are found!"

The children were carried home. Everyone was very happy.

Tom sat on his bed and told of their escape.

He had looked this way. And then he had looked that way. Suddenly he saw a light which he thought was day-light. He found a hole in the rock and could see the river. When he told Becky she didn't believe him at first. But when she saw the light and the river she was very happy.

They found some men on the river and told their story. At first the men did not believe the children.

But then they believed the children and took them to a house where they were given food and could rest, before being taken home.

It was several days before Tom and Becky were strong again.

Tom heard that Huck was ill and went to visit him.

Mrs. Douglas would not let Tom talk about his story to Huck, because Huck was not strong enough to listen. Also, she would not let the boys talk about what had happened at her house on Cardiff Hill. Tom learned about that at home. He also heard that Indian Joe's friend had been found in the river. He had died in the river while trying to run away.

About two weeks later, Tom visited Becky at her home. Mr. Thatcher and some friends were there.

They asked Tom if he wished to go into the cave again.

Tom said yes.

"Maybe other people wish to go, also." Mr. Thatcher said. "But I had the entrance closed with a metal door. It can't be opened. No one will get lost in that cave again."

"Oh, no," Tom said, "Indian Joe is in there!"

31
What Happened to Indian Joe

Soon everyone heard the news. In a few minutes men were in boats on their way to the cave. Tom was in a boat with Mr. Thatcher.

The door was opened. Indian Joe was on the ground, dead. Tom could understand how Indian Joe had felt.

But he felt happy.

The next morning, Tom and Huck talked.

Now Huck told Tom about following Indian Joe up the hill to Mrs. Douglas's house.

"Indian Joe came from hotel Number Two," Huck said. "Now we shall never find the box of money."

"Huck," Tom said, "that money was never in the hotel. It is in the cave! Will you go there with me and help to bring it out?"

"I will as long as we do not get lost."

"Are you strong enough?" Tom asked.

"I can't walk far, Tom."

"I will take you there in a boat. It will be easy for you."

"I want to start now, Tom."

Tom agreed. "We want some bread and meat, two bags, some thread and some lights."

They went in a friend's boat. One entrance was closed but Tom knew another entrance.

The boys entered the hole. They tied the thread to a rock to guide their return. After a few steps they found the small, beautiful river. Tom was afraid. He told Huck that this was where he and Becky got lost.

The boys walked very quietly.

They continued walking and soon they came to a place where the floor ended.

Tom said: "Now I will show you something, Huck." He held his light high. "What can you see?

On the big rock?"

"Tom, it is a cross!"

"That is where I saw Indian Joe, Huck. And where is Number Two? Remember what he said? 'Under the cross.'"

Huck was afraid. "Tom, I want to leave."

"What! And leave the money?"

"Yes. Leave it. Indian Joe's ghost is there."

"No, Huck. It is near the door, where he died. That is far away."

"No, Tom. His ghost would be with the money. I know about these things."

"No Huck, it would not be near a cross."

Huck agreed. "You are right Tom. We must find the box."

The boys climbed down the great rock. Tom went first, and Huck followed.

Near the great rock, the boys found where some person had been eating and sleeping. But they found no money.

They looked and found some old wood under

some rocks. Behind the old wood was a small entrance. They went in.

"Huck, look there!"

It was the box of money. There were also two guns.

"We have it!" said Huck, putting his hands on the pieces of gold. "We are rich, Tom!"

"Huck, I was always sure that we would get the money. And we have it."

They put the money in two bags, and carried it back to the river.

They left the guns to get another day.

It was dark when they arrived at the village.

"Huck," said Tom, "we will take the money to Mrs. Douglas's house. I know a place near there to leave it tonight."

They borrowed a cart and took the bags of money to Cardiff Hill.

Near Mr. Jones's house they stopped to rest. Mr. Jones came out. "Who is there?" he said.

"Huck and Tom Sawyer."

"Come with me, boys. Everyone is waiting for you. Let me help. Your cart is very heavy. But it's not full of money, I am sure!"

They entered Mrs. Douglas's house.

All the important people of the village were there. The Thatcher family, the Harper family, Aunt Polly, Sid, Mary, and many more. All were dressed in their best clothes.

Tom and Huck were very dirty. Aunt Polly's face was red when she saw Tom's face and clothes.

Mrs. Douglas took the boys to a bedroom and said: "Wash and dress now. Here are new clothes for both of you. Come and join the others when you are ready."

32

Mr. Jones's Surprise is Not a Surprise

Huck said, "Tom, we can run away. We can go through the window."

"Why do you want to run away?"

"I can't join so many people, Tom."

"Don't worry. I will take care of you."

Sid came into the room.

"Sid, why are all these people here?"

"Old Mr. Jones has a surprise. It is about Huck following Indian Joe and the other man to this house. But most people already know. Someone told them." He laughed.

"I know who that was," Tom said, looking at Sid.

Some minutes later Huck and Tom were eating at a big table with the others. Then Mr. Jones stood up to speak. He told the story about Huck. It was true that people did not look surprised. But people tried to look surprised.

Mrs. Douglas thanked Huck again and again. She said that she would give Huck a room in her house, and send him to school, and that later she would give him money to start a business.

Tom said, "Huck won't need it. He is rich."

People tried not to laugh.

Tom said, "Huck has money. I can show you." He ran outside.

Tom entered, carrying the heavy bags. He opened them and let the yellow gold fall out on the table. "Look!" he said. "Half is Huck's and half is mine."

Everyone looked. No one could speak.

Then they asked Tom to explain.

It was a long story, but everyone was interested.

There was more than twelve thousand dollars. Some of the village people owned land and were much richer than Tom and Huck. But no one had ever seen so much money at one time.

33

Tom Makes New Plans

Tom's and Huck's money was a great thing in the poor little village. Everyone talked about it. No one could believe it.

People went looking for more money. They looked in every old, empty house.

Every word Tom and Huck spoke became important. The village newspaper had a story about Tom and Huck and everyone wanted to be friends with them.

Mrs. Douglas put Huck's money in a bank. Mr. Thatcher did the same with Tom's. Each boy had money to spend now. He had almost a dollar for every day of the year. In those days, a dollar a week was enough to buy a boy's food and clothes, and send him to school.

Mr. Thatcher liked Tom because he had saved Becky from the cave. He thought Tom would become a great man.

Huck Finn's life had changed. It was almost too great for him. Mrs. Douglas had taken him into her home. She kept him clean. Every night he had to sleep in a clean bed. He had to eat like a gentleman. He had to go to church.

He tried his new life for three weeks, and then the next day he was gone. Mrs. Douglas and all the people in the village tried to find him. They were afraid that he had died in the river.

Early on the third morning Tom Sawyer went to an old building outside the village. He found Huck. Huck had been sleeping in the building. He sat there now, smoking. His hair was wild. He was wearing his old, dirty clothes. But he looked happy.

Tom asked him to go home to Mrs. Douglas.

Huck's face became sad. He said, "Do not talk about it, Tom. I tried it. It is not for me. She is good to me, and friendly. But I can't live with her.

I must get up at the same time every morning. I must wash. I must sleep in a bed. I must wear those good clothes. I can't move in those clothes. I can't sit down, I can't run, I can't play on the ground in them. I must go to church. I must wear shoes on Sunday."

"We all live like that, Huck."

"Tom, I am different. I can't live like that. It is too easy to get food. Mrs. Douglas won't let me smoke. And she prays all the time. I had to leave, Tom or I would die. And when school begins, I would have to go to school.

"Tom, being rich is no good. I wish I was dead all the time. I like these old clothes. I like sleeping in this place. This is what I want. Tom, I will give you my share of the money. You can give me money when I need it. But not often. I do not like what is easy to get. Please explain to Mrs. Douglas."

"Oh, Huck, you know that I can't do that. And if you try longer, you will like it."

"Like it? Yes, I will like it as if I sat on a fire! No, Tom, I won't be rich and I won't live in a house. I like the forest and the river and a place like this for sleeping. But now we are rich and all our games, like being pirates, have stopped."

"Listen, Huck. Being rich won't change that."

"Is that true, Tom?"

"It is true. But if you want to join me and the other boys and be in my club, you must live like us."

"Tom, that's not friendly."

"I want you to join us, Huck. But all the boys who join Tom Sawyer's Club must be good, kind people."

Huck was quiet. He was thinking. After a while he said, "I will return to Mrs. Douglas for a month. I will try, if you will let me be in Tom Sawyer's Club."

"I agree, Huck. Come with me now. And I promise to ask Mrs. Douglas to change a little, Huck."

"Will you, Tom? That is good. When will you start your club?"

"Oh, soon. This evening we can have the first meeting."

"What will we do at the meeting?"

"We will promise always to help each other, and promise never to tell what we plan to do, and promise to kill any person who hurts one of us."

"I like that, Tom. I like it."

"And we must make those promises at night, in a quiet place outside the village. And sign with blood."

"This is better than being a pirate, Tom. I will stay with Mrs. Douglas. And we will have so much fun that everyone in the village will talk about us. And then Mrs. Douglas will be happy because she took me into her home."

A Few Words to End

So ends this story. Because it is the history of a boy, it must stop here. It could not go much further without becoming the history of a man.

Most of the people in this book are still living, and are happy. Some day the story may continue. But for now, it will stop.

Word List

・本文で使われている全ての語を掲載しています（LEVEL 1、2）。ただし、LEVEL 3 以上は、中学校レベルの語を含みません。
・語形が規則変化する語の見出しは原形で示しています。不規則変化語は本文中で使われている形になっています。
・一般的な意味を紹介していますので、一部の語で本文で実際に使われている品詞や意味と合っていないことがあります。
・品詞は以下のように示しています。

名 名詞	代 代名詞	形 形容詞	副 副詞	動 動詞	助 助動詞
前 前置詞	接 接続詞	間 間投詞	冠 冠詞	略 略語	俗 俗語
熟 熟語	頭 接頭語	尾 接尾語	記 記号	関 関係代名詞	

A

□ **a** 冠①1つ[人]の, ある ②～につき

□ **able** 形《be – to》(人が)～することができる

□ **about** 副およそ～, 約～ 前①～について ②～のまわりに[の] 形 be about to ～ ～しようとしている

□ **above** 前①～の上に ②～より以上で 副①上に ②以上に

□ **across** 前～を渡って, ～の向こう側に 副渡って, 向こう側に

□ **action** 名①行動, 活動 ②動作, 行為 ③機能, 作用

□ **adventure** 名冒険 動危険を冒す

□ **afraid** 形①心配して ②恐れて, 怖がって **I'm afraid (that)** ～ 残念ながら～, 悪いけれど～ **be afraid of** ～ ～を恐れる **be afraid to** ～ こわくて～できない

□ **after** 前～のあとに[で], ～の次に 副あとに[で] 接（～した）あとに[で] **run after** ～を追いかける

□ **afternoon** 名午後 **Good afternoon.** こんにちは。

□ **again** 副再び, もう一度 **again and again** 何度も繰り返して

□ **against** 前①～に対して, 反対して ②～に不利な

□ **age** 名①年齢 ②時代, 年代

□ **ago** 副～前に **long ago** ずっと前に, 昔

□ **agree** 動①～に同意する ②～と意見が一致する

□ **ahead** 副①前方へ[に] ②前もって **Go ahead.** かかってきな。

□ **air** 名①《the –》空中, 空間 ②空気, 《the –》大気 ③雰囲気, 様子

□ **Alfred** 名アルフレッド《人名》

□ **all** 形すべての 代全部, すべて(のもの[人]) **all the time** 明けても暮れても **not ～ at all** 少しも[全然]～ない 名全体

□ **almost** 副ほとんど, もう少しで(～するところ)

□ **alone** 形ただ1人の 副1人で, ～だけで

□ **along** 前～に沿って 副前へ, ずっと, 進んで **come along** やって来る, 現れる **walk along** (前へ)歩く

□ **already** 副すでに, もう

□ **also** 副～も(また), ～も同様に 接その上, さらに

□ **always** 副いつも, 常に **as always** いつものように

□ **am** 動 ～である，（～に）いる［ある］

□ **among** 前（3つ以上のもの）の間で［に］，～の中で［に］

□ **Amy** 名 エイミイ《人名》

□ **an** 冠 ①1つ［人］の，ある ②～につき

□ **and** 接 ①そして，～と… ②《同じ語を結んで》ますます ③《結果を表して》それで，だから

□ **angry** 形 怒って，腹を立てて

□ **animal** 名 動物 形 動物の

□ **another** 形 ①もう1つ［1人］の ②別の 代 ①もう1つ［1人］ ②別のもの

□ **answer** 動 ～に答える，～に応じる 名 答え，応答，返事

□ **any** 形 ①《疑問文で》何か，いくつかの ②《否定文で》何も，少しも（～ない）③《肯定文で》どの～も 代 ①《疑問文で》（～のうち）何か，どれか，誰か ②《否定文で》少しも，何も［誰も］～ない ③《肯定文で》どれも，誰でも 副 少しは，少しも

□ **anyone** 代 ①《疑問文，条件節で》誰か ②《否定文で》誰も（～ない）③《肯定文で》誰でも

□ **anything** 代 ①《疑問文で》何か，どれでも ②《否定文で》何も，どれも（～ない）③《肯定文で》何でも，どれでも 副 いくらか

□ **appear** 動 ①現れる，見えてくる ②（～のように）見える，～らしい

□ **apple** 名 リンゴ

□ **are** 動 ～である，（～に）いる［ある］

□ **arm** 名 腕 **put one's arms around**（人）の肩［腕・胴体］に両手をまわす

□ **around** 副 ①まわりに，あちこちに ②およそ～，約～ **jump around** 跳び回る **put one's arms around**（人）の肩［腕・胴体］に両手をまわす 前 ～のまわりに，～のあちこちに

□ **arrive** 動 ①～に到着する ②～に到達する

□ **as** 接 ①《as ～ as …の形で》…と同じくらい～ ②～のとおりに，～のように ③～しながら，～しているときに ④～するにつれて，～にしたがって ⑤～なので ⑥～だけれども **as if ～** まるで～のように **as long as ～する以上は，～である限りは** 前 ①～として（の）②～のとき 副 同じくらい 代 ①～のような ②～だが

□ **ask** 動 ①～を尋ねる，～を聞く ②～を頼む，～を求める **ask for ～** ～を求める

□ **asleep** 形 眠って（いる状態の）副 眠って，休止して

□ **at** 前 ①《場所・時》～に［で］②《目標・方向》～に［を］，～に向かって

□ **ate** 動 eat（～を食べる）の過去

□ **aunt** 名 おば

□ **away** 副 離れて，遠くに，去って **carry away** 運び去る **go away** 立ち去る **look away** 横を向く **move away** ①立ち去る ②移す，動かす **pull away** もぎ取る **take away** 取り上げる **turn away** 横を向く **walk away** 立ち去る

B

□ **baby** 名 ほん坊

□ **back** 名 ①背中 ②裏，後ろ 副 ①戻って ②後ろへ［に］形 裏の，後ろの **fall on its back** 仰向けに倒れる **go back to**（中断していた作業に）再び取り掛かる **turn one's back towards** ～の方に背を向ける

□ **bad** 形 ①悪い，下手な ②気の毒な **That's too bad.** 残念だ。

□ **bag** 名 袋，かばん

□ **ball** 名 ボール，球

□ **bang** 名 ドスン・バタンという音

□ **bank** 名 ①銀行 ②堤防，岸

□ **be** 動 ～である，（～に）いる［ある］，～となる 助 ①《現在分詞とともに用

A
B
C
D
E
F
G
H
I
J
K
L
M
N
O
P
Q
R
S
T
U
V
W
X
Y
Z

137

いて》〜している ②《過去分詞とと
もに用いて》〜される、〜されている
be to 〜 〜することになっている
hadn't been to school 学校に行っ
ていなかった

□ **beard** 图あごひげ

□ **beautiful** 形美しい、すばらしい

□ **became** 動 become（〜になる、〜
に似合う）の過去

□ **because** 接（なぜなら）〜だから、
〜という理由[原因]で

□ **Becky** 图ベッキー《人名》

□ **become** 動〜になる

□ **bed** 图①ベッド、寝所 **get into
bed** ベッドに入る **go to bed** 床に
つく、寝る ②花壇、川床、土台

□ **bedroom** 图寝室

□ **been** 動 be（〜である）の過去分詞

□ **beetle** 图甲虫、カブトムシ

□ **before** 前〜の前に[で]、〜より以
前に 接〜する前に 副以前に **the
night before** 前の晩

□ **began** 動 begin（始まる[始める]）
の過去

□ **begin** 動始まる[始める]、起こる

□ **behind** 前〜の後ろに、〜の背後に
副後ろに、背後に

□ **believe** 動〜を信じ（てい）る

□ **Ben** 图ベン《人名》

□ **Benjamin** 图ベンジャミン《人名》

□ **best** 形最もよい、最大[多]の 副
最もよく、最も上手に

□ **better** 形①よりよい ②（人が）回
復して 副①よりよく、より上手に
②むしろ **had better 〜** 〜するほう
がよい

□ **between** 前（2つのもの）の間に
[で、の] **between 〜 and …** 〜と…
の間に[で、の] 副間に

□ **bible** 图聖書

□ **big** 形①大きい ②偉い、重要な

□ **bill** 图①請求書、勘定書 ②法案 ③

紙幣

□ **Billy** 图ビリー《人名》

□ **bird** 图鳥

□ **bit** 图①《a 〜 of 〜》少しの〜、1つ
の〜 ②小片 **a bit** 少し、ちょっと
動 bite（〜をかむ）の過去、過去分詞

□ **black** 形黒い、有色の 图黒、黒色

□ **blood** 图血、血液

□ **blue** 形青い 图青（色）

□ **boat** 图ボート、小舟、船

□ **boat-men** 图 boat-man（（貸し）
ボート屋、ボートの漕ぎ手、船頭）の
複数

□ **body** 图体、死体、胴体

□ **bone** 图骨、《-s》骨格

□ **book** 图①本、書物 ②《the B-》聖
書

□ **borrow** 動（〜を）借りる

□ **both** 形両方の、2つともの 副《both
〜 and … の形で》〜も…も両方とも
代両方[者]、双方

□ **bought** 動 buy（〜を買う）の過去、
過去分詞

□ **box** 图箱、容器

□ **boy** 图少年、男の子 **my boy**（親し
い）友達《呼びかけ》

□ **bread** 图①パン ②食物、生計

□ **break** 動①〜を壊す、折る ②（記
録、法律、約束）を破る

□ **bright** 形①輝いている、鮮明な ②
快活な 副輝いて、明るく

□ **bring** 動①〜を持ってくる、〜を
連れてくる ②〜をもたらす、生ずる
bring out（物）をとりだす、引き出す

□ **broken** 動 break（〜を壊す）の過
去分詞 形①破れた、壊れた ②落胆
した ③破産した

□ **brother** 图①兄弟 ②同僚、同胞

□ **brought** 動 bring（〜を持ってく
る、〜をもたらす）の過去、過去分詞

□ **brush** 图①ブラシ ②絵筆 動〜に

ブラシをかける, ～を払いのける

□ **build** 動～を建てる, ～を確立する 名①体格, 構造 ②《-ing》建物, ビル

□ **built** 動 build（～を建てる）の過去, 過去分詞 形～づくりの, ～の体格の

□ **burn** 動燃える[燃やす], 日焼けする[させる] 名やけど, 日焼け

□ **business** 名①職業, 仕事 ②商売

□ **busy** 形忙しい

□ **but** 接①でも, しかし ②～を除いて 前～を除いて, ～のほかは 副ただ, のみ, ほんの

□ **buy** 動～を買う, ～を獲得する

□ **by** 前①《位置》～のそばに[で] ②《手段・方法・行為者・基準》～によって, ～で ③《期限》～までには ④《通過・経由》～を経由して, ～を通って 副そばに, 通り過ぎて

C

□ **cake** 名①菓子, ケーキ ②固まり 動固まる

□ **call** 動①～を呼ぶ, 叫ぶ ②～に電話をかける ③立ち寄る **call to** ～に声をかける

□ **came** 動 come（来る, 起こる, ～になる）の過去

□ **can** 助①～できる ②～してもよい ③～であり得る ④《否定文で》～のはずがない **Can I ～?** ～してもよいですか? **Can you ～?** ～してくれますか?

□ **candy** 名キャンディー, 甘いもの

□ **Cardiff Hill** 名カーディフ・ヒル《地名》

□ **care** 名心配, 注意 **take care of ～** ～の世話をする, ～に気をつける 動①《通例否定文, 疑問文で》気にする, 心配する ②世話をする **care for ～** が好きである, 愛情を持つ

□ **careful** 形注意深い, 慎重な

□ **carry** 動①～を運ぶ, ～を連れていく, ～を持ち歩く ②伝わる[伝える] **carry away** ①運び去る ②心を奪う

□ **cart** 名荷馬車, 荷車 動～を運ぶ

□ **case** 名①事件, 問題, 事柄 ②実例, 場合 ③実状, 状況, 症状 **in case** ～だといけないので

□ **cat** 名ネコ

□ **catch** 動①～をつかまえる ②～に追いつく ③偶然つかむ, 引っかかる

□ **caught** 動 catch（～をつかまえる, ～に追いつく）の過去, 過去分詞

□ **cave** 名洞穴, 洞くつ

□ **chair** 名いす

□ **chance** 名①偶然, 運 ②好機 ③見込み 形偶然の, 思いがけない

□ **change** 動①変わる[変える] ②交換する 名変化, 変更

□ **child** 名子供

□ **children** 名 child（子供）の複数

□ **choose** 動～を選ぶ, ～に決める

□ **Christ** 名イエス＝キリスト

□ **church** 名教会, 礼拝（堂）

□ **cigarette** 名（紙巻）たばこ

□ **clean** 形①きれいな, 清潔な ②正当な 動～を掃除する 副①きれいに ②全く, すっかり

□ **climb** 動（～を）登る, 徐々に上がる 名登ること, 上昇

□ **close** 形①近い ②親しい ③狭い 副①接近して ②密集して 動①閉まる[閉める] ②～を終える, 閉店する

□ **clothes** 名衣服, 身につけるもの

□ **club** 名クラブ, (同好)会

□ **coat** 名コート 動①～の表面を覆う ②～に上着を着せる

□ **cold** 形①寒い, 冷たい ②冷淡な, 冷静な 名①寒さ, 冷たさ ②風邪

□ **come** 動①来る, 行く, 現れる ②(出来事が)起こる, 生じる ③～になる **come along** やって来る, 現れる **come down** ～を下りて来る **come**

139

out 現れる **There comes a time in every boy's life** すべての少年の人生の中で～な時期がやってくる

☐ **Connecticut** 图コネチカット州《地名》

☐ **continue** 動続く[続ける], (中断後)再開する

☐ **cook** 動～を料理する, (食物が)煮える 图料理人, コック

☐ **cool** 形涼しい, 冷えた 動涼しくなる, 冷える **cool down** 冷ます, 涼しくする

☐ **could** 助can (～できる)の過去 **Could you ～?** ～してくださいますか?《ていねいな依頼》**could have done** ～だったかもしれない《仮定法》

☐ **count** 動①～を数える ②～を(…と)みなす ③重要[大切]である

☐ **country** 图①国 ②《the –》田舎, 郊外

☐ **course** 图①進路, 方向 ②経過, なりゆき **of course** もちろん, 当然

☐ **cross** 動～を横切る, わたる 图十字架, 十字形のもの

☐ **cry** 動泣く, ～と叫ぶ, 大声を出す 图泣き声, 叫び, かっさい

☐ **cut** 動①～を切る, ～を刈る ②～を短縮する, ～を削る

D

☐ **dark** 形①暗い, 闇の ②(色が)濃い ③陰うつな 图①《the –》暗がり, 闇 ②《無冠詞で》日暮れ, 夜 ③暗い色[影]

☐ **daughter** 图娘

☐ **David** 图《聖書》ダビデ《人名》**David and Goliath** ダビデとゴリアテ

☐ **day** 图①日中, 昼間 ②日, 期日

☐ **day-light** 图日光, 昼の明かり

☐ **dead** 形①死んでいる, 活気のない ②全くの 图《the –》死者たち, 故人 **spirits of the dead** 死者の魂

☐ **dear** 形いとしい, 親愛なる～ 图ねえ, あなた《呼びかけ》間まあ, おや

☐ **decide** 動～を決定[決意]する, ～しようと決める, 判決を下す

☐ **deep** 形①深い, 深さ～の ②深遠な ③濃い 副深く

☐ **destroyer** 图破壊者

☐ **devil** 图①悪魔(のような人) ②やっかいなこと **talk of devils** うわさをすれば影《ことわざ》

☐ **diary** 图日記

☐ **did** 助動do (《否定文・疑問文をつくる》, ～をする)の過去

☐ **die** 動死ぬ, 消滅する

☐ **different** 形異なった, 違った, 別の, さまざまな

☐ **difficult** 形困難な, 難しい, 扱いにくい

☐ **dinner** 图①ディナー, 夕食 ②夕食[食事]会, 祝宴

☐ **dirty** 形①汚い, よごれた ②卑劣な, 不正な 動(～を)汚す

☐ **discover** 動～を発見する, ～に気づく

☐ **do** 助①《ほかの動詞とともに用いて現在形の否定文・疑問文をつくる》②《同じ動詞をくり返すかわりに用いる》③《動詞を強調するのに用いる》動～をする

☐ **doctor** 图医者, 博士(号)

☐ **does** 助動do (《否定文・疑問文をつくる》, ～をする)の3人称単数現在

☐ **dog** 图犬

☐ **dollar** 图ドル《米国などの通貨単位。記号 $》

☐ **done** 動do (～をする)の過去分詞

☐ **door** 图①ドア, 戸 ②一軒, 一戸

☐ **Douglas** 图ダグラス《人名》

☐ **down** 副①下へ, 降りて, 低くなっ

て ②倒れて 前〜の下方へ, 〜を下
って 形下方の, 下りの **come down**
〜を下りて来る **cool down** 冷ます,
涼しくする **look down at** 〜に目[視
線]を落とす

□ **draw** 動①引く[引かれる] ②〜を
描く ③引き分けになる[する]

□ **dream** 名夢, 幻想 動(〜の)夢を
見る, 夢想[想像]する

□ **dress** 名ドレス, 衣服, 正装 動①
服を着る[着せる] ②〜を飾る

□ **drink** 動飲む, 飲酒する 名飲み物,
酒, 1杯

□ **drop** 動(ぽたぽた)落ちる[落と
す], 下がる[下げる] 名しずく, 落下

□ **drunk** 動drink(飲む)の過去分詞
形(酒に)酔った, 〜に酔いしれて
get drunk 酔っ払う

□ **dry** 形①乾燥した ②辛口の 動乾
燥する[させる], 〜を干す

□ **during** 前〜の間(ずっと)

□ **dying** 動die(死ぬ, 消滅する)の現
在分詞 形死にかかっている, 消えそ
うな **be dying for**〜 しきりに〜し
たがっている

E

□ **each** 形それぞれの, 各自の 代そ
れぞれ, 各自 **each other** お互いに
副それぞれに

□ **ear** 名耳, 聴覚

□ **early** 形①(時間や時期が)早い ②
初期の, 幼少の, 若い 副早く, 早めに

□ **earth** 名①《the‐》地球 ②大地,
陸地, 土 ③この世

□ **easy** 形①やさしい, 簡単な ②気楽
な, くつろいだ

□ **eat** 動〜を食べる, 食事する

□ **eaten** 動eat(〜を食べる)の過去
分詞

□ **eleven** 名①11(の数字), 11人[個]

②11人のチーム, イレブン 形11の,
11人[個]の

□ **empty** 形①空の, 空いている ②
(心などが)ぼんやりした, 無意味な
動空になる[する], 注ぐ

□ **end** 名①終わり, 終末 ②果て, 末,
端 ③目的 動終わる[終える]

□ **engage** 〜を約束する, 〜と婚
約する

□ **enjoy** 動〜を楽しむ

□ **enough** 形十分な, (〜するに)足
る 名十分(な量・数), たくさん 副(〜
できる)だけ, 十分に, 全く

□ **enter** 動①(〜に)入る, 入会[入学]
する[させる] ②〜を記入する

□ **entrance** 名①入り口, 入場 ②開
始

□ **escape** 動(〜から)逃げる, 免れる,
もれる 名逃亡, 脱出, もれ

□ **even** 副①《強意》〜でさえも, 〜で
すら, いっそう, なおさら **get even**
復讐する

□ **evening** 名①夕方, 晩 ②《the‐
またはone's‐》末期, 晩年, 衰退期

□ **ever** 副①今までに, これまで, かつ
て ②《強意》いったい

□ **every** 形①どの〜も, すべての, あ
らゆる ②毎〜, 〜ごとの

□ **everyone** 代誰でも, 皆

□ **everything** 代すべてのこと[も
の], 何でも, 何もかも

□ **everywhere** 副どこにいても, い
たるところに

□ **excite** 動興奮する[させる]

□ **experience** 名経験, 体験 動〜
を経験[体験]する

□ **explain** 動〜を説明する, 〜を明
らかにする, 〜を釈明[弁明]する

□ **eye** 名目, 視力 **eye to eye** 目と目
が合う

141

F

☐ **face** 名①顔, 顔つき ②外観, 外見 動〜に直面する, 〜に立ち向かう

☐ **fall** 動落ちる, 倒れる **fall at one's foot** (人)の足元にひざまずく **fall on** 〜に降りかかる **fall on its back** 仰向けに倒れる **fall out** 落ちる, 飛び出す 名①落下, 墜落 ②滝 ③秋

☐ **family** 名家族, 家庭, 一門, 家柄

☐ **famous** 形有名な, 名高い

☐ **far** 副遠くに, はるかに, 離れて

☐ **farm** 名農場, 農家

☐ **fast** 形(速度が)速い 副速く, 急いで

☐ **father** 名父親

☐ **favorite** 名お気に入り(の人[物]) 形お気に入りの, ひいきの

☐ **feel** 動〜を感じる, 〜と思う 名《-ing》①感じ, 気持ち ②触感, 知覚 ③同情, 思いやり, 感受性 形《-ing》感じる, 感じやすい, 情深い

☐ **feet** 名①foot (足)の複数

☐ **fell** 動fall (落ちる, (値段・温度が)下がる)の過去

☐ **felt** 動feel (〜を感じる)の過去, 過去分詞

☐ **fence** 名囲み, さく

☐ **few** 形①ほとんど〜ない, 《a−》少しは〜ある, 2, 3の 代少数の人[物]

☐ **fight** 動〜と戦う, 争う 名①戦い, 争い ②闘志, ファイト

☐ **fill** 動満ちる[満たす]

☐ **find** 動①〜を見つける ②〜とわかる ③〜を得る

☐ **fine** 形①元気な ②美しい, りっぱな ③晴れた ④結構な, 快適な 副りっぱに, 申し分なく

☐ **finger** 名(手の)指 動指でさわる

☐ **finish** 動終わる[終える] 名終わり, 最後

☐ **Finn** 名フィン《人名》

☐ **fire** 名①火, 炎, 火事 ②砲火, 攻撃 動①〜を発射する ②〜を解雇する ③火をつける

☐ **first** 名最初, 第1(の人)[物]) 形①第1の, 最初の ②最も重要な 副第1に, 最初に

☐ **fish** 名魚 動釣りをする

☐ **five** 名5(の数字), 5人[個] 形5の, 5人[個]の

☐ **floor** 名床, 階

☐ **flower** 名花, 草花

☐ **fly** 動飛ぶ[飛ばす]

☐ **follow** 動①〜についていく ②〜の結果として起こる ③(忠告など)に従う ④〜を理解できる

☐ **food** 名食物, えさ, 肥料

☐ **foot** 名足, 足どり

☐ **for** 前①《目的・原因・対象》〜にとって, 〜のために[の], 〜に対して ②《期間》〜間 ③《代理》〜の代わりに ④《方向》〜へ(向かって)

☐ **forest** 名森林

☐ **forget** 動〜を忘れる, 〜を置き忘れる

☐ **forgot** 動forget (〜を忘れる)の過去, 過去分詞

☐ **found** 動find (〜を見つける, 〜とわかる)の過去, 過去分詞

☐ **four** 名4(の数字), 4人[個] 形4の, 4人[個]の

☐ **fourth** 名第4番目(の人・物), 4日 形第4番目の

☐ **friend** 名友だち, 仲間

☐ **friendly** 形親しみのある, 親切な, 友情のこもった 副友好的に, 親切に

☐ **from** 前①《出身・出発点・時間・順序・原料》〜から ②《原因・理由》〜がもとで **from 〜 to …** 〜から…まで

☐ **front** 名正面, 前 **in front of 〜** 〜の前に 形正面の, 前面の

☐ **full** 形①満ちた, いっぱいの, 満期

の ②完全な, 盛りの, 充実した **full of life** 元気いっぱいで, 活発な

□ **fun** 名楽しみ, 冗談, おもしろいこと 動からかう, ふざける

□ **further** 形いっそう遠い, その上の, なおいっそうの 副いっそう遠く, その上に, もっと 動〜を促進する

□ **future** 名未来, 将来 形未来の, 将来の

G

□ **game** 名ゲーム, 試合, 遊び, 競技

□ **garden** 名庭, 〜園

□ **gardening** 名園芸 **gardening thing** 園芸用具

□ **gate** 名門, とびら, 入り口

□ **gave** 動give (〜を与える, 〜を伝える) の過去

□ **gentleman** 名紳士

□ **get** 動①〜を得る, 〜を手に入れる ②(ある状態に) なる, いたる ③〜がわかる, 〜を理解する ④〜させる **get home** 家に着く[帰る] **get into bed** ベッドに入る **get on top** 上に乗る **get out** 外に出る **get to** (事) を始める

□ **ghost** 名幽霊

□ **girl** 名女の子, 少女

□ **girl-friend** 名女友だち, 愛人, 恋人

□ **give** 動①〜を与える, 〜を贈る ②〜を伝える, 〜を述べる ③〜をする **give up** あきらめる, 降参する

□ **given** 動give (〜を与える, 〜を伝える) の過去分詞 形与えられた

□ **glad** 形うれしい, 喜んで (〜する)

□ **go** 動①行く, 出かける ②動く ③進む, 経過する, いたる ④(ある状態に) なる **Go ahead.** かかってきな。 **go away** 立ち去る **go back to** (中断していた作業に) 再び取り掛かる

□ **gold** 名金, 金貨, 金製品, 金色 形金の, 金製の, 金色の

□ **gold-colored** 形金色に着色された

□ **Goliath** 名《聖書》ゴリアテ《人名》ダビデに殺された巨人の名

□ **gone** 動go (行く, 進む, (ある状態に) なる) の過去分詞 形去った

□ **good** 形よい, 上手な, 優れた

□ **goodness** 名①善良さ, よいところ ②優秀 ③神《婉曲表現》

□ **got** 動get (〜を得る) の過去・過去分詞

□ **Gracie** 名グレイシー《人名》

□ **grave** 名墓

□ **graveyard** 名墓地

□ **gray** 名①灰色の ②どんよりした, 憂うつな 名灰色

□ **great** 形①大きい, 広大な, (量や程度が) たいへんな ②偉大な, 優れた ③すばらしい, おもしろい

□ **grew** 動grow (成長する, 増大する) の過去

□ **ground** 名地面, 土 **on the ground** 地面に 動①〜を基づかせる ②着陸する 形(粉に) ひいた, すった

□ **group** 名集団, 群 動集まる

□ **guide** 動〜を (道) 案内する, (人) を導く 名ガイド, 手引き, 入門書

□ **gun** 名銃, 大砲 動〜を銃で撃つ

□ **Guy of Guisborne** ガイ卿, ギズボーンのガイ《人名。『ロビン・フッド』より》

H

□ **had** 動have (〜を持つ, 〜がある[いる]) の過去, 過去分詞 助haveの過去《過去完了の文をつくる》 **had better 〜** 〜したほうがよい

□ **hair** 名髪, 毛

□ **half** 名半分 形半分の, 不完全の

A
B
C
D
E
F
G
H
I
J
K
L
M
N
O
P
Q
R
S
T
U
V
W
X
Y
Z

副 半分, なかば, 不十分に

□ **hand** 名①手,（時計の）針 ②援助の手, 助け 動 ～を手渡す

□ **hang** 動 かかる[かける], ～をつるす, ぶら下がる ～を絞首刑にする

□ **happen** 動①（出来事が）起こる, 生じる ②偶然[たまたま]～する

□ **happy** 形 幸せな, うれしい, 幸運な, 満足して

□ **hard** 形①堅い ②激しい, 難しい 副①一生懸命に ②激しく ③堅く

□ **Harper** 名 ハーパー《人名》

□ **has** 動 help have（～を持つ, ～がある[いる],《現在完了の文をつくる》）の3人称単数現在

□ **hat** 名（縁のある）帽子

□ **have** 動①～を持つ[持っている], ～を抱く ②～がある[いる] ③～を食べる[飲む] ④～を経験する,（病気に）かかる ⑤～を催す, ～を開く **have to ～** ～しなければならない **don't have to ～** ～する必要はない 助《〈have＋過去分詞〉の形で》～した, ～したことがある, ずっと～している ⑥《〈have＋事＋過去分詞〉の形で》（事）を～してもらう

□ **he** 代 彼は[が]

□ **head** 名 頭 **stand on one's head to make** ～するためにできる限りのことをする 動 ～に向かう, ～へ向ける

□ **health** 名 健康（状態）, 衛生, 保健

□ **hear** 動 ～を聞く, ～が聞こえる **hear of** ～について聞く

□ **heard** 動 hear（～を聞く）の過去, 過去分詞

□ **heart** 名①心臓, 胸 ②心, 感情, ハート ③中心, 本質

□ **heavy** 形 重い, 激しい, つらい

□ **held** 動 hold（～をつかむ, ～を保つ,（会などを）開く）の過去, 過去分詞

□ **hello** 間 こんにちは, やあ

□ **help** 動①～を助ける, ～を手伝う ②～を給仕する 名 助け, 手伝い

□ **her** 代①彼女を[に] ②彼女の

□ **here** 副 ここに[で] 名 ここ

□ **HF** 略 ハックルベリー・フィンのイニシャル

□ **high** 形①高い ②気高い, 高価な 副①高く ②ぜいたくに 名 高い所

□ **hill** 名 丘, 塚

□ **him** 代 彼を[に]

□ **himself** 代 彼自身

□ **his** 代①彼の ②彼のもの

□ **history** 名 歴史, 経歴

□ **hit** 動①～を打つ, なぐる, ～をぶつける ②～に命中する 名①打撃 ②命中 ③大成功

□ **hold** 動①～をつかむ, ～を持つ, 抱く ②～を保つ, 持ちこたえる ③（会などを）開く

□ **hole** 名①穴, すきま ②苦難, 困難 動 穴をあける, 穴に入る[入れる]

□ **holiday** 名 祝祭日, 休暇 形①休日[休暇]の ②よそ行きの, 楽しい

□ **home** 名 家, 故郷, 家庭 副 家に **get home** 家に着く[帰る] **on one's way home** 帰り道で **take him into her home** 彼を自分の家に引き取る

□ **homework** 名 宿題, 予習

□ **hope** 名 希望, 期待, 見込み 動（～を）望む, ～であるようにと思う

□ **Hoss** 名 ホス《人名》

□ **hot** 形①暑い, 熱い ②できたての, 新しい ③からい, 強烈な, 熱中した 副①熱く ②激しく

□ **hotel** 名 ホテル, 旅館

□ **hour** 名 1時間, 時間

□ **house** 名①家, 家庭 ②（特定の目的のための）建物, 小屋

□ **how** 副①どうやって, どれくらい, どんなふうに ②なんて（～だろう） **How about ～?** ～はどうですか?

how to ~ ～する方法, どうやって～するか

- [ ] **Huck** 名 ハック《人名》
- [ ] **Huckleberry** 名 ハックルベリー《人名》
- [ ] **hug** 名 抱きしめること 動 しっかりと抱きしめる
- [ ] **human** 形 人間の, 人の 名 人間
- [ ] **hundred** 名 ① 100（の数字）, 100人［個］ ②何百, 多数 形 ① 100の, 100人［個］の ②多数の
- [ ] **hungry** 形 ①空腹の, 飢えた ②渇望して ③不毛の
- [ ] **hunt** 動 ～を狩る, 狩りをする, ～を捜し求める 名 狩り, 追跡
- [ ] **hurry** 動 急ぐ［急がせる］, あわてる 名 急ぐこと, 急ぐ必要 **in a hurry** 急いで
- [ ] **hurt** 動 ～を傷つける, 痛む, ～を害する 名 傷, けが, 苦痛, 害
- [ ] **husband** 名 夫

I

- [ ] **I** 代 私は［が］
- [ ] **idea** 名 考え, 意見, アイデア, 計画
- [ ] **if** 接 もし～ならば, たとえ～でも, ～かどうか 名 疑問, 条件, 仮定
- [ ] **ill** 形 ①病気の, 不健康な ②悪い 副 悪く, 不完全に
- [ ] **important** 形 重要な, 大切な, 有力な
- [ ] **in** 前 ①《場所・位置・所属》～（の中）に［で, の］ ②《時》～（のとき）に［の, で］, ～後（に）, ～の間（に） ③《方法・手段》～で ④《服装》～を身につけて, ～を着て 副 中［内］へ［に］
- [ ] **Indian** 名 （アメリカ）インディアン 形 （アメリカ）インディアンの
- [ ] **inside** 名 内部, 内側 形 内部［内側］にある 副 内部［内側］に 前 ～の内部［内側］に

- [ ] **instead** 副 その代わりに **instead of ~** ～の代わりに, ～をしないで
- [ ] **interest** 名 ①興味, 関心 ②利害（関係）, 利益 ③利子, 利息 動 ～に興味を起こさせる 形 **be interested in ~** ～に興味［関心］がある
- [ ] **into** 前 ①《動作・運動の方向》～の中へ［に］ ②《変化》～に［へ］
- [ ] **is** 動 ～である, （～に）いる［ある］
- [ ] **island** 名 島
- [ ] **it** 代 ①それは［が］, それを［に］ ②《天候・日時・距離・寒暖などを示す》
- [ ] **its** 代 それの, あれの

J

- [ ] **jail** 名 刑務所
- [ ] **Jeff** 名 ジェフ《人名》
- [ ] **Jesus Christ** 名 イエス・キリスト
- [ ] **Jim** 名 ジム《人名》
- [ ] **job** 名 仕事, 職
- [ ] **Joe** 名 ジョー《人名》
- [ ] **John** 名 ジョン《人名》
- [ ] **join** 動 ①一緒になる, 参加する ②連結［結合］する［させる］ 名 結合
- [ ] **Jones** 名 ジョーンズ《人名》
- [ ] **judge** 動 （～に）判決を下す, 裁く, 判断する 名 裁判官, 判事, 審査員
- [ ] **jump** 動 跳ぶ, 跳躍する, ～を飛び越える **jump around** 跳び回る 名 ①跳躍 ②急騰, 急転
- [ ] **just** 形 正しい, もっともな, 当然な 副 ①ちょうど, （～した）ばかり ②ほんの, 単に, ただ～だけ ③ちょっと

K

- [ ] **kept** 動 keep（～をとっておく, ～を守る）の過去, 過去分詞
- [ ] **kill** 動 （～を）殺す, ～を消す 名 殺

すこと

- □ **killing** 图殺すこと, 殺害
- □ **kind** 形親切な, 優しい 图種類, 本質
- □ **kiss** 图キス 動～にキスする
- □ **knew** 動 know（～を知っている[知る]）の過去
- □ **knife** 图ナイフ, 小刀, 包丁, 短剣
- □ **know** 動①～を知っている[知る], ～がわかる, ～を理解している ②～と知り合いである

L

- □ **lady** 图婦人, ～夫人, 奥さん
- □ **lake** 图湖, 湖水
- □ **land** 图陸地, 土地 動上陸する, 着陸する
- □ **large** 形①大きい, 広い ②大勢の, 多量の 副①大きく ②自慢して
- □ **last** 形①《the –》最後の ②この前の, 先～ ③最新の 副①最後に ②この前 图最後（のもの）, 終わり 動続く, 持ちこたえる
- □ **late** 形①遅い, 後期の ②最近の ③故～ 副①遅れて ②最近まで, 以前
- □ **later** 形もっと遅い, もっとあとの 副あとで, 後ほど
- □ **laugh** 動笑う **laugh at ～** ～を見て[聞いて]笑う 图笑い（声）
- □ **law** 图①法, 法律 ②弁護士業, 訴訟
- □ **Lawrence** 图ローレンス《人名》
- □ **lead** 動①～を導く, 案内する ②（生活）を送る 图①鉛 ②先導, 指導
- □ **leader** 图指導者, リーダー
- □ **learn** 動（～を）学ぶ, 習う, 教わる, 知識［経験］を得る
- □ **leave** 動①出発する, ～を去る ②～を残す ③（人）を～のままにしておく ④～をゆだねる 图①休暇 ②（～する）許可 ③別れ
- □ **leaves** 图 leaf（葉）の複数 動 leave

（出発する, ～を残す）の3人称単数現在

- □ **left** 图《the –》左, 左側 形左の, 左側の 副左に, 左側に 動 leave（出発する, ～を残す）の過去, 過去分詞
- □ **leg** 图脚, すね, 支柱
- □ **less** 形～より小さい[少ない] 副～より少なく, ～ほどでなく 图より少ない数[量・額]
- □ **let** 動（人など）に～させる[～するのを許す], ～を（ある状態に）する **Let's ～.** （一緒に）～しましょう。**let go** 離す
- □ **letter** 图①手紙 ②文字
- □ **lie** 動①うそをつく ②横たわる, 寝る ③（ある状態に）ある, 存在する 图うそ, 詐欺
- □ **life** 图①生命, 生物 ②一生, 生涯, 人生 ③生活, 暮らし, 世の中 **for one's life** 必死で **full of life** 元気いっぱいで, 活発な **There comes a time in every boy's life** すべての少年の人生の中で～な時期がやってくる
- □ **light** 图光, あかり 動火をつける, （～を）照らす, 明るくする 形①明るい ②（色が）薄い, 淡い ③軽い, 容易な 副軽く, 容易に
- □ **like** 動（～を）好む, （～が）好きである 副～に似ている, ～のような 形似ている, ～のような, ～しそうで 接あたかも～のように
- □ **listen** 動聞く, 耳を傾ける **listen to ～** ～を聞く
- □ **little** 形①小さい, 幼い ②少しの, 短い ③ほとんど～ない, 《a –》少しはある 图少し（しか）ない, 少量 副全然～ない, 《a –》少しはある
- □ **live** 動住む, 生きている 形《-ing》①生きている, 現存の ②生き生きした 图《-ing》①生活, 生存 ②暮らし, 生計
- □ **long** 形長い, 長期の 副長い間, ずっと **no longer ～** もはや～でない[～しない] **so [as] long as ～** ～する限りは

□ **look** 動①見る ②〜に見える，〜の顔つきをする ③注意する ④ほら，ねえ **look after** 〜の世話をする **look away** 横を向く **look down at** 〜に目［視線］を落とす **look for** 〜を探す **look like** 〜のように見える **look out** 外を見る

□ **lost** 動 lose（〜を失う，〜に負ける）の過去，過去分詞 形①失った，負けた ②道に迷った，困った

□ **lot** 名①くじ，運 ②地所，区画 ③**a lot of** 〜［**lots of** 〜］たくさんの〜

□ **loud** 形 大声の，騒がしい 副 大声に［で］

□ **loudly** 副 大声で，騒がしく

□ **love** 名 愛，愛情，思いやり 動（〜を）愛する，恋する，〜が大好きである

□ **loving** 形 愛情のある，愛情に満ちた

M

□ **mad** 形①気の狂った ②逆上した，理性をなくした ③ばかげた ④（〜に）熱狂［熱中］して，夢中の

□ **made** 動 make（〜を作る）の過去，過去分詞 形 作った，作られた

□ **make** 動①〜を作る，〜を得る ②〜を行なう，〜になる ③〜を（…に）する，〜を…させる **make a man = make a picture of a man**《省略》

□ **man** 名 男性，（男の）人

□ **many** 形 多数の，たくさんの 名 多数（の人［物］）

□ **mark** 名①印，記号，跡 ②点数 ③特色 動①〜に印［記号］をつける ②採点する ③〜を目立たせる

□ **marry** 動（〜と）結婚する

□ **Mary** 名 メアリー，メリー《人名》

□ **may** 助①〜かもしれない ②〜してもよい，〜できる **May I 〜?** 〜してもよいですか? 名《M-》5月

□ **maybe** 副 たぶん，おそらく

□ **me** 代 私を［に］

□ **mean** 動①〜を意味する ②〜のつもりで言う，〜を意図する

□ **meat** 名 肉

□ **meet** 動①〜に会う，〜と知り合いになる ②合流する，交わる 名《-ing》集会，会見，会議

□ **meeting-house** 名 教会堂，公会堂，礼拝堂

□ **men** 名 man（男性）の複数

□ **met** 動 meet（〜に会う，合流する）の過去，過去分詞

□ **metal** 名 金属，合金

□ **might** 助①〜かもしれない ②〜してもよい，〜できる

□ **Miller** 名 ミラー《人名》

□ **million** 名①100万，《-s》数百万もの人［物］ ②たくさん 形①100万の ②多数の

□ **mine** 代 私のもの 名 鉱山

□ **minute** 名①（時間の）分 ②ちょっとの間

□ **miss** 動①〜を失敗する，〜を免れる ②〜がないのに気づく，（人）がいなくて寂しく思う 名①はずれ，失敗 ②《M-》《女性に対して》〜さん

□ **Mississippi River** 名 ミシシッピ川

□ **money** 名 金，通貨

□ **month** 名 月，1カ月

□ **more** 形①もっと多くの ②それ以上の，余分の 副 もっと，さらに多く，いっそう 名 もっと多くの物［人］

□ **morning** 名 朝，午前

□ **most** 形①最も多い ②たいていの，大部分の 名①大部分，ほとんど ②最多数 副 最も（多く）

□ **mother** 名 母親

□ **mouth** 名①口 ②言葉，発言

□ **move** 動①動く［動かす］ ②〜を感動させる ③引っ越す，移動する **move away** ①立ち去る ②移す，動

かす **move in** 引っ越す

- □ **Mr.** 名《男性に対して》～さん, ～氏
- □ **Mrs.** 名《結婚している女性に対して》～さん, ～夫人
- □ **much** 形 (量・程度が) 多くの, 多量の 副①とても, たいへん ②ほぼ
- □ **Muff** 名 マフ《人名》
- □ **must** 助①～しなければならない ②～に違いない 名 絶対に必要なこと [もの]
- □ **my** 代 私の **my boy** (親しい) 友達《呼びかけ》
- □ **myself** 代 私自身

N

- □ **name** 名①名前 ②名声 動①～に名前をつける ②名前を名乗る
- □ **narrow** 形①狭い ②限られた 動狭くなる [する]
- □ **near** 前～の近くに, ～のそばに 形近い, 親しい 副近くに, 親密で
- □ **need** 動～を必要とする, ～が必要である 助～する必要がある
- □ **neighbor** 名 隣人, 隣り合うもの 動 (～に) 隣接する
- □ **never** 副決して [少しも] ～ない, 一度も～ない
- □ **new** 形①新しい, 新規の ②新鮮な, できたての 名《-s》ニュース, 報道, 便り, 記事
- □ **newspaper** 名 新聞 (紙)
- □ **next** 形①次の, 翌～ ②隣の 副①次に ②隣に 代 次の人 [物] 前～の次に, ～の隣に [の]
- □ **nice** 形 すてきな, よい, きれいな, 親切な
- □ **night** 名 夜, 晩 **the night before** 前の晩
- □ **nine** 名 9 (の数字), 9人 [個] 形 9の, 9人 [個] の

- □ **no** 副①いいえ, いや ②少しも～ない 形～がない, 少しも～ない, ～どころでない, ～禁止 名 拒否
- □ **nobody** 代 誰も [1人も] ～ない 名 とるに足らない人
- □ **noon** 名 正午, 真昼
- □ **no-one** 代 誰も [1人も] ～ない
- □ **normal** 形 普通の, 平均の, 標準的な 名 平常, 標準, 典型
- □ **nose** 名 鼻, 嗅覚, におい
- □ **not** 副～でない, ～しない
- □ **nothing** 代 何も～ない [しない]
- □ **now** 副①今 [現在] (では) ②今すぐに ③では, さて 名 今, 現在
- □ **number** 名①数, 数字, 番号 ②～号, ～番

O

- □ **o'clock** 副～時
- □ **of** 前①《所有・所属・部分》～の, ～に属する ②《性質・特徴・材料》～の, ～製の ③《部分》～のうち ④《分離・除去》～から
- □ **off** 副①離れて ②はずれて ③止まって ④休んで **take off** ～を取り除く 形①離れて ②季節はずれの ③休みの 前～を離れて, ～をはずれて, (値段が) ～引きの
- □ **often** 副 しばしば, たびたび
- □ **oh** 間 ああ, おや, まあ
- □ **OK** 形《許可, 同意, 満足などを表して》よろしい, 正しい 名 許可, 承認 動～をオーケー [承認] する
- □ **old** 形①年とった, 老いた ②～歳の ③古い, 昔の 名 昔, 老人
- □ **on** 前①《場所・接触》～ (の上) に ②《日・時》～に ③《関係・従事》～に関して, ～について, ～して 副 前へ, 続けて **on one's way home** 帰り道で **on one's way** 途中で **on which** = when

□ **once** 副①一度, 1回 ②かつて 名一度, 1回 **at once** すぐに, 同時に 接いったん~すると 形かつての

□ **one** 名①1（の数字）, 1人[個] 形①1 の, 1人[個]の ②ある~ ③《the-》唯一の 代①《一般の》人, ある物 ②一方, 片方 **one by one** ひとつずつ, ひとりずつ

□ **only** 形唯一の 副単に, ~にすぎない 接ただし, だがしかし

□ **open** 形①開いた, 広々とした ②公開された 動①（~を）開く, 広がる[広げる] ②~を打ち明ける

□ **or** 接①~か…, または ②さもないと ③すなわち, 言い換えると

□ **order** 名①順序 ②整理, 整とん ③命令, 注文（品） 動①~に（…するよう）命じる, ~を注文する ②~を整とんする

□ **other** 形①ほかの, 異なった ②《2つのうち》もう一方の, 《3つ以上のうち》残りの 代①ほかの人[物], 《the-》残りの1つ 副そうでなく, 別に

□ **our** 代私たちの

□ **out** 副①外へ[に], 不在で, 離れて ②世に出て ③消えて ④すっかり 形①外の, 遠く離れた, ②公表された **bring out**（物）をとりだす, 引き出す **come out** 現れる **fall out** 落ちる, 飛び出す **get out** 外に出る **look out** 外を見る **step out** 外へ出る **take out** 取り出す **take out of** ~から出す **throw out** 放り出す **walk out of** ~から出る **way out** 出口, 逃げ道

□ **outside** 名外部, 外側 形外部の, 外側の 副外へ, 外側に 前~の外に[で, の, へ], ~の範囲を越えて

□ **over** 前①~の上の[に], ~を一面におおって ②~を越えて, ~以上に, ~よりまさって ③~の向こう側の[に] ④~の間 副①上に, 一面に, ずっと ②終わって, すんで

□ **own** 形自身の 動~を持っている, ~を所有する

□ **owner** 名持ち主, オーナー

P

□ **page** 名ページ

□ **pain** 名①痛み, 苦悩 ②《-s》骨折り, 苦労 動~に苦痛を与える, 痛む

□ **painkiller** 名鎮痛剤

□ **paint** 動①~にペンキを塗る, ~を（絵の具などで）描く 名塗料, ペンキ, 絵の具

□ **paper** 名①紙 ②新聞, 論文, 答案 ③《-s》書類 ④紙幣, 手形

□ **part** 名①部分, 割合 ②役目 動（~を）分ける, （~と）別れる

□ **pass** 動①（~のそばを）過ぎる[通る] ②（年月が）たつ

□ **peace** 名①平和, 和解 ②平穏, 静けさ **at peace** 平和に, 安らかに, 心穏やかで

□ **pen** 名①ペン ②文筆, 文体 ③囲い, おり 動~を囲い[おり]に入れる

□ **people** 名（一般に）人々

□ **person** 名①人 ②人格, 人柄

□ **Peter** 名ピーター《人名》

□ **pick** 動①（~を）突く, つついて穴をあける, ほじくり出す ②（~を）つみとる, 選ぶ **pick up** ①持ち上げる, 拾い上げる ②引き取る, 受け取る ③片付ける

□ **picnic** 名ピクニック

□ **picture** 名絵, 写真, 《-s》映画 **make a picture** 絵を描く

□ **piece** 名①一片, 部分 ②~個 **in two pieces** 2つに

□ **pirate** 名海賊 動海賊行為を働く

□ **place** 名①場所, 建物 ②余地, 空間 動~を置く, ~を（…に）任じる

□ **plan** 名計画, 設計（図）, 案 動~を計画する

□ **play** 動①遊ぶ, 競技する ②（楽器）

を演奏する, (〜の役)を演じる 名遊
び, 競技, 劇

□ **please** 動〜を喜ばす, 〜を満足さ
せる 副どうぞ

□ **pocket** 名①ポケット, 袋

□ **policeman** 名警察官

□ **Polly** 名ポリー《人名》

□ **poor** 形①貧しい, 貧弱な ②劣った,
下手な ③不幸な

□ **Potter** 名ポッター《人名》

□ **pray** 動祈る, 懇願する **pray for**
〜のために祈る

□ **present** 形①出席している, ある,
いる ②現在の 名①《the－》現在 ②
贈り物 動①〜を紹介する ②現れる
③〜を提出する, 〜を与える

□ **president** 名①大統領 ②社長,
(大学の)学長, 頭取

□ **pretend** 動①〜のふりをする,
〜を装う ②あえて〜しようとする
pretend to 〜 〜するふりをする

□ **prison** 名①刑務所, 監獄 ②監禁

□ **problem** 名問題, 難問

□ **promise** 名①約束 ②有望 動①
(〜を)約束する ②〜の見込みがある
make a promise 約束する

□ **pull** 動①(〜を)引く, 引っ張る ②
〜を引きつける **pull away** もぎ取る

□ **push** 動(〜を)押す, 押し進む[押
し進める] 名押し, 突進, 後援

□ **put** 動①〜を置く, 〜を載せる ②
〜を入れる, 〜をつける ③〜を(あ
る状態)にする **put on** (服を)着る
put one's arms around (人)の肩
[腕・胴体]に両手をまわす

Q

□ **question** 名質問, 疑問, 問題

□ **quick** 形(動作が)速い, すばやい
副速く, 急いで, すぐに

□ **quickly** 副速急に, 急いで

□ **quiet** 形①静かな, 穏やかな, じっ
とした ②おとなしい, 無口な, 目立
たない 名静寂, 平穏 動静まる[静
める]

□ **quietly** 副①静かに ②平穏に, 控
えめに

R

□ **raft** 名いかだ

□ **rain** 名雨, 降雨 動①雨が降る ②
雨のように降る[降らせる]

□ **ran** 動 run (走る, 運行する, (川が)
流れる, 〜を経営する)の過去

□ **read** 動(〜を)読む, 読書する

□ **ready** 形用意[準備]ができた, ま
さに〜しようとする 副用意して

□ **real** 形実際の, 実在する, 本物の
名《the－》実体, 実在するもの

□ **really** 副本当に, 実際に, 確かに

□ **receive** 動(〜を)受けとる, 〜を
もらう

□ **red** 形赤い 名赤, 赤色

□ **red-handed** 形現行犯の

□ **remember** 動〜を思い出す, 〜を
覚えている, 〜を忘れないでいる

□ **report** 動①(〜を)報告[通知]す
る ②〜を記録する, 〜の記事を書く
名①報告 ②(新聞の)記事, 報道

□ **rest** 名①休息 ②安静 ③休止, 停止
④残り 動①休む, 眠る ②休止する,
静止する ③(〜に)基づいている

□ **result** 名結果, 成り行き, 成績 動
(結果として)起こる[生じる], 結局
〜になる

□ **return** 動帰る, 戻る, 〜を返す

□ **rich** 形富んだ, 金持ちの, 豊かな,
濃い, 深い

□ **ride** 動(〜に)乗る, (〜に)乗って
いく

□ **right** 形①正しい ②適切な ③健全
な ④右(側)の 副①まっすぐに ②

150

右(側)に ③ちょうど, 正確に

□ **rise** 動①昇る, 上がる ②生じる
名①上昇, 上がること ②発生

□ **river** 名川

□ **river-bank** 名川岸, 川の土手

□ **river-boat** 名川船

□ **road** 名①道路, 道, ～通り ②手段,
方法

□ **Robin Hood** 名ロビン・フッド《人
名》

□ **Robinson** 名ロビンソン《人名》

□ **rock** 名岩, 岸壁, 岩石

□ **Rogers** 名ロジャーズ《人名》

□ **room** 名部屋

□ **run** 動①走る, 逃げる ②(川が)流
れる **run after** ～を追いかける **run
away** 逃げる, 走り去る

S

□ **sad** 形①悲しい, 悲しげな ②惨め
な, 不運な

□ **sadly** 副悲しそうに, 不幸にも

□ **safe** 形①安全な, 危険のない ②用
心深い, 慎重な 名金庫

□ **said** 動 say (言う)の過去, 過去分詞

□ **same** 形①同じ, 同様の ②前述の
代《the－》同一人[物] 副《the－》
同様に

□ **sang** 動 sing (歌う)の過去

□ **sat** 動 sit (座る)の過去, 過去分詞

□ **Saturday** 名土曜日

□ **save** 動①(～を)救う, ～を守る
②～をとっておく, ～を節約する

□ **saw** 動① see (～を見る, ～に会う)
の過去 ②のこぎりを使う 名のこぎり

□ **Sawyer** 名ソーヤー《人名》

□ **say** 動言う, 口に出す 名言うこと,
言い分 間さあ, まあ

□ **school** 名①学校, 校舎 **hadn't**

been to school 学校に行っていなか
った

□ **sea** 名《the－》海, ～海

□ **seat** 名席, 座席, 位置

□ **second** 名①第2(の人[物]) ②(時
間の)秒, 瞬時 形第2の, 2番の 副
第2に

□ **see** 動①～を見る, ～が見える ②
～とわかる ③～に会う ④～を確か
める, ～を調べる ⑤～に気をつける

□ **seen** 動 see (～を見る, ～に会う)
の過去分詞

□ **sell** 動売る, (～で)売れる

□ **send** 動①～を送る, 届ける ②手
紙を出す ③(人)を～に行かせる

□ **sent** 動 send (～を送る)の過去, 過
去分詞

□ **several** 形①いくつかの ②めいめ
いの 名数人[個]

□ **shall** 助～するでしょう, ～でしょ
う **Shall I ～?** (私が)～しましょう
か? **Shall we ～?** (一緒に)～しま
しょうか?

□ **share** 名①分け前, 分担 ②株 動
～を分配する, ～を共有する

□ **she** 代彼女は[が]

□ **Sherwood Forest** 名シャーウ
ッドの森

□ **ship** 名船, 飛行船

□ **shirt** 名ワイシャツ, ブラウス

□ **shoe** 名《-s》くつ

□ **shoot** 動①(銃)を撃つ ②～を放
つ, 噴出する

□ **short** 形①短い ②背の低い ③不
足している 副①手短に, 簡単に ②
不足して

□ **shot** 名①発砲, 銃撃 ②弾丸
動 shoot (撃つ)の過去, 過去分詞

□ **should** 助～すべきである, ～し
たほうがよい **should never have
done** ～すべきではなかった(のにし
てしまった)《仮定法》

151

□ **shout** 動叫ぶ, 大声で言う, どなりつける 名叫び, 大声, 悲鳴

□ **show** 動①～を見せる, ～を示す, 見える ②～を明らかにする, ～を教える ③～を案内する 名①表示, 見世物 ②外見, 様子

□ **sick** 形①病気の ②むかついて, 嫌気がさして **feel sick** 気分が悪い, 吐き気がする

□ **Sid** 名シッド, シド《人名》

□ **sign** 名①きざし, 徴候 ②あと ③記号 ④身ぶり, 合図, 看板 動①署名する ②～に合図する

□ **silly** 形愚かな, 思慮のない 名馬鹿者

□ **sing** 動（歌を）歌う

□ **sir** 名①あなた, 先生《目上の男性, 客などに対する呼びかけ》②拝啓《手紙の書き出し》**Dear Sir** 拝啓

□ **sister** 名①姉妹, 姉, 妹 ②修道女

□ **sit** 動座る, 腰掛ける, 位置する **sit down** 座る

□ **six** 名6（の数字）, 6人[個] 形6の, 6人[個]の

□ **skin** 名皮膚

□ **sky** 名空, 天空, 大空

□ **sleep** 動①眠る, 寝る ②活動しない 名①睡眠, 冬眠 ②静止, 不活動

□ **slow** 形遅い 副遅く, ゆっくりと 動遅くする[なる]

□ **slowly** 副遅く, ゆっくり

□ **small** 形①小さい, 少ない ②取るに足りない 副小さく, 細かく

□ **smile** 動微笑する, にっこり笑う 名微笑, ほほえみ

□ **smoke** 動喫煙する, 煙を出す 名①煙, 煙状のもの ②《-ing》喫煙

□ **so** 副①とても ②同様に, ～もまた **so～(that)**… とても～なので… 接①だから, それで ②では, さて **so that** ～するために 代そう, そのとおり

□ **sold** 動sell（売る）の過去, 過去分詞

□ **some** 形①いくつかの, 多少の ②ある, 誰か, 何か 代①いくつか ②ある人[物]たち

□ **someone** 代ある人, 誰か

□ **something** 代①ある物, 何か ②いくぶん, 多少

□ **sometimes** 副ときどき

□ **son** 名息子, 子弟, ～の子

□ **song** 名歌, 詩歌, 鳴き声

□ **soon** 副まもなく, すぐに, すみやかに

□ **sorry** 形気の毒に[申し訳なく]思う, 残念な

□ **sound** 名音, 騒音, ひびき **make a sound** 音を出す 動①音がする[鳴る] ②（～のように）思われる, （～と）聞こえる

□ **speak** 動話す, 言う, 演説する **speak of ～** ～を話題にする

□ **special** 形①特別の, 特殊の, 臨時の ②専門の

□ **spend** 動①（金など）を使う, 浪費する ②（時）を過ごす

□ **spirit** 名①霊 ②精神, 気力 **spirits of the dead** 死者の魂

□ **spoke** 動speak（話す）の過去

□ **Sprague** 名スプレイグ《人名》

□ **stab** 動～を刺す

□ **stand** 動①立つ[立たせる], 立っている, ある ②～に耐える, ～に立ち向かう **stand on one's head to make** ～するためにできる限りのことをする **stand up** 立ち上がる

□ **start** 動出発する, 始まる[始める], 生じる[生じさせる] 名出発, 開始

□ **state** 名①有様, 状態 ②《the-》国家, （アメリカなどの）州 動～を述べる 形国家の

□ **stay** 動①とどまる, 泊まる, 滞在する ②持続する, ～のままでいる

□ **steal** 動①～を盗む ②こっそりと手に入れる[動く] 名盗み, 盗品

□ **step** 名①歩み, 1歩 (の距離) ② 段階 ③踏み段, 階段 動歩む, 踏む **step out** 外へ出る

□ **still** 副①まだ, 今でも ②それでも (なお) 形静止した, 静かな

□ **stood** 動 stand (立つ [立たせる], ~に耐える) の過去, 過去分詞

□ **stop** 動①やめる [やめさせる] ② 立ち止まる

□ **storm** 名①嵐, 暴風雨 ②強襲 動 ①~を襲撃 [強襲] する ②嵐が吹く

□ **story** 名①物語, 話 ②階

□ **straight** 形①一直線の, まっすぐ な, 直立 [垂直] の ②率直な, 整然と した 副①一直線に, まっすぐに, 垂 直に ②率直に

□ **strange** 形①知らない, 見 [聞き] 慣れない ②奇妙な, 変わった ③落ち つかない

□ **stranger** 名①見知らぬ人, 他人 ②不案内 [不慣れ] な人

□ **street** 名①街路 ②~通り

□ **strong** 形強い, 堅固な, 強烈な 副 強く, 猛烈に

□ **student** 名学生, 生徒

□ **study** 動 (~を) 勉強 [研究] する 名①勉強, 研究 ②書斎

□ **succeed** 動①成功する ②(~の) 跡を継ぐ

□ **such** 形①そのような, このような ②そんなに, とても ③《such ~ as ま たは such as ~の形で》~のような, ~するような 代そのような人 [物]

□ **suddenly** 副突然, 急に

□ **summer** 名夏

□ **sun** 名《the ~》太陽, 日

□ **Sunday** 名日曜日

□ **Sunday school** 名 (教会の) 日 曜学校

□ **sunny** 形①日当たりのよい, 日の さす ②陽気な, 快活な

□ **sun-tanned** 形日焼けした

□ **sure** 形確かな, 確実な, 必ず~する 副確かに, 全く, 本当に **make sure** よく確かめる

□ **surprise** 動~を驚かす 名驚き, 不意打ち

□ **Suzy** 名スージー《人名》

□ **swim** 動泳ぐ 名泳ぎ

T

□ **table** 名テーブル, 食卓, 台 動~ を卓上に置く, ~をたな上げにする

□ **take** 動①~を取る, ~を持つ ② ~を持って [連れて] いく, ~を捕ら える ③~に乗る **take away** 取り上 げる **take from** ~から引く, 選ぶ **take him into her home** 彼を自分 の家に引き取る **take off** ~を取り除 く **take out of** ~から出す **take out** 取り出す

□ **taken** 動 take (~を取る, ~を持っ て [連れて] いく, ~に乗る, (時間・労 力) を費やす) の過去分詞

□ **talk** 動話す, 語る, 相談する **talk of** ~のことを話す **talk of devils** う わさをすれば影《ことわざ》

□ **tall** 形高い, 背の高い

□ **taste** 名①味, 風味 ②好み, 趣味 動~の味がする, (~を) 味わう

□ **teach** 動 (~を) 教える 名《-ing》 ①教授, 授業 ②《-ings》教え, 教訓

□ **teacher** 名先生, 教師

□ **tear** 名①涙 ②裂け目 動~を裂く, ~を破る

□ **tell** 動①(~を) 話す, 言う, 語る ② ~を教える, ~に知らせる, ~に伝え る ③~がわかる

□ **temple** 名寺, 神殿

□ **ten** 名 10 (の数字), 10人 [個] 形 10 の, 10人 [個] の

□ **than** 接~よりも

□ **thank** 動~に感謝する, ~に礼を

言う 名《-s》感謝, 謝意

□ **that** 形その, あの 副そんなに, それほど 代①それ, あれ, その[あの] 人[物] ②〜である… 接〜ということ, 〜なので, 〜だから **so that** 〜できるように **so 〜 that** … 非常に〜なので…

□ **Thatcher** 名サッチャー《人名》

□ **the** 冠①その ②《形容詞の前で》〜な人々

□ **their** 代彼(女)らの, それらの

□ **them** 代彼(女)らを[に], それらを[に]

□ **then** 副そのとき(に[は]), それから, 次に 名そのとき

□ **there** 副①そこに[で, の], そこへ, あそこへ ②《 – is[are]》〜がある[いる] **up there** あそこで

□ **these** 代これら, これ 形これらの, この

□ **they** 代①彼(女)らは[が], それらは[が] ②(一般の)人々は[が]

□ **thing** 名①物, 事 ②《-s》事情, 事柄 ③人, やつ

□ **think** 動(〜と)思う, (〜と)考える **think of 〜** 〜について考える

□ **third** 名第3(の人・物) 形第3の, 3番の

□ **this** 形①この, こちらの ②今〜 代これ, この人[物]

□ **Thomas** 名トマス《人名》

□ **those** 形それらの, あれらの 代それら[あれら]の人[物]

□ **thought** 名考え, 意見 動think ((〜と)思う)の過去, 過去分詞

□ **thousand** 名①1000(の数字), 1000人[個] ②何千, 多数 形①1000の, 1000人[個]の ②多数の

□ **thread** 名糸, 糸のように細いもの

□ **three** 名3(の数字), 3人[個] 形3の, 3人[個]の

□ **threw** 動throw((〜を)投げる)の過去

□ **through** 前〜を通して, 〜中を[に], 〜中 副①通して, 〜中 ②全く, すっかり

□ **throw** 動〜を投げる **throw out** 放り出す

□ **ticket** 名切符, 乗車[入場]券

□ **tie** 動〜を結ぶ, 〜を束縛する 名①結び(目) ②ネクタイ ③《-s》縁

□ **time** 名①時, 時間, 歳月 ②時期 **all the time** 明けても暮れても **There comes a time in every boy's life** すべての少年の人生の中で〜な時期がやってくる

□ **tire** 動疲れる[疲れさせる], 飽きる[飽きさせる] 名(車の)タイヤ

□ **to** 前①《方向・変化》〜へ, 〜に, 〜のほうへ ②《程度・時間》〜まで ③《適合・付加・所属》〜に ④《 – ＋動詞の原型》〜するために[の], 〜する, 〜すること

□ **today** 名今日 副今日(で)は

□ **together** 副一緒に, ともに

□ **told** 動tell((〜を)話す, 言う)の過去, 過去分詞

□ **Tom** 名トム《人名》

□ **tomorrow** 名明日 副明日(は)

□ **tonight** 名今夜, 今晩 副今夜(は)

□ **too** 副①〜も(また) ②あまりに〜すぎる, とても〜 **too 〜 to** … …するには〜すぎる

□ **took** 動take(〜を取る, 〜を持って[連れて]いく, 〜に乗る, (時間・労力)を費やす)の過去

□ **tool** 名道具, 用具, 工具

□ **top** 名頂上, 首位 **get on top** 上に乗る

□ **tore** 動tear(〜を裂く, 〜を引き離す)の過去

□ **torn** 動tear(〜を裂く, 〜を引き離す)の過去分詞

□ **touch** 動①触れる, さわる ②接触する ③〜を感動させる 名①接触, 手ざわり ②手法

154

□ **toward** 前①《運動の方向・位置》〜のほうへ，〜に向かって ②《目的》〜のために

□ **towards** 前①《運動の方向・位置》〜のほうへ，〜に向かって ②《目的》〜のために

□ **town** 名町，都会，都市

□ **toy** 名おもちゃ 動遊ぶ

□ **travel** 動①旅行する ②進む，移動する［させる］，伝わる 名旅行，運行

□ **tree** 名①木，木製のもの ②系図

□ **tried** 動 try（〜しようと試みる）の過去，過去分詞

□ **trouble** 名①困難，迷惑 ②心配，苦労 ③もめごと **get into trouble** 問題を起す **in trouble** 面倒な状況で，困って

□ **true** 形①本当の，本物の，真の ②誠実な，確かな 副真実に，純粋に

□ **trust** 動信用［信頼］する，委託する 名信用，信頼，委託

□ **truth** 名①真理，事実，本当 ②誠実，忠実さ

□ **try** 動〜をやってみる，〜しようと試みる 名試み，ためし

□ **TS** 略トム・ソーヤーのイニシャル

□ **turn** 動①〜をひっくりかえす，回転する［させる］，曲がる［曲げる］，向かう［向ける］ ②〜になる，〜に変える **turn away** 横を向く **turn one's back towards** 〜の方に背を向ける

□ **Turner** 名ターナー《人名》

□ **twelve** 名12（の数字），12人［個］ 形12の，12人［個］の

□ **two** 名2（の数字），2人［個］ 形2の，2人［個］の **in two pieces** 2つに

U

□ **under** 前①《位置》〜の下［に］ ②《状態》〜で，〜を受けて，〜のもと ③《数量》〜未満の，〜より下の 形下の，下部の 副下に［で］，従属［服従］して

□ **understand** 動〜を理解する，〜がわかる 名《-ing》①理解（力），会得 ②知力，分別 ③一致，了解

□ **unhappy** 形不運な，不幸な

□ **unite** 動①〜を1つにする［なる］，合わせる，結ぶ ②結束する［させる］

□ **until** 前〜まで（ずっと） 接〜のときまで，〜するまで

□ **up** 副①上へ，上がって，北へ ②立って，近づいて ③向上して，増して 前①〜の上（のほう）へ，高いほうへ ②（道）に沿って 形上向きの，上りの **stand up** 立ち上がる **up there** あそこで **walk up** 歩み寄る

□ **us** 代私たちを［に］

□ **USA** 略アメリカ合衆国（the United States of America の略）

□ **use** 動①〜を使う ②〜を費やす 名使用，用途 **of use** 役に立って 形①《be -d to》〜に慣れている ②《-d》中古の 助《-d to》（以前は）よく〜したものだった

□ **useful** 形役に立つ，有効な，有益な

□ **usually** 副ふつう，いつも（は）

V

□ **verse** 名詩，詩の1行，(聖書の)節

□ **very** 副とても，非常に，全く 形本当の，きわめて，まさしくその

□ **village** 名村，村落

□ **visit** 動（人）を訪問する 名訪問

□ **voice** 名①声，音声 ②意見，発言権

W

□ **wait** 動①待つ ②延ばす［延ばせる］，遅らせる **wait for 〜** 〜を待つ

□ **wake** 動①目がさめる，起きる［起

A
B
C
D
E
F
G
H
I
J
K
L
M
N
O
P
Q
R
S
T
U
V
W
X
Y
Z

こす] ②奮起する **wake up** 起きる, 目が覚める, (人を) 起こす

□ **walk** 動歩く [歩かせる], 散歩する [させる] 名歩くこと, 散歩 **go for a walk** 散歩に行く **walk along** (前へ) 歩く **walk away** 立ち去る **walk on one's hand** 逆立ちして歩く **walk out of** ~から出る **walk up** 歩み寄る

□ **wall** 名①壁, へい ②障壁

□ **want** 動~がほしい, ~を望む, ~したい [~してほしい] 名欠乏, 不足

□ **warm** 形①暖かい, 温暖な ②思いやりのある, 愛情のある 動暖まる [暖める]

□ **wart** 名①いぼ ②(木の) こぶ

□ **was** 動~であった, (~に) いた [あった]

□ **wash** 動①(~を) 洗う, 洗濯する ②押し流す [される] 名洗うこと

□ **watch** 動①~をじっと見る, ~を見物する ②~に注意 [用心] する, ~を監視する

□ **water** 名①水 ②(川, 湖, 海などの) 多量の水

□ **way** 名①道, 通り道 ②方向, 距離 ③方法, 手段 ④習慣 **on one's way** 途中で **on one's way home** 帰り道で **way out** 出口, 逃げ道

□ **we** 代私たちは [が]

□ **weak** 形①弱い, 力のない, 病弱な ②劣った, 下手な, 苦手な

□ **wear** 動①~を着ている ②疲れる, 消耗する, すり切れる

□ **week** 名週, 1週間

□ **well** 副①うまく, 上手に ②十分に, よく, かなり **as well** なおその上 副へえ, まあ, ええと 形健康な, 適当な, 申し分ない

□ **went** 動 go (行く, 進む, (ある状態に) なる) の過去

□ **were** 動~であった, (~に) いた [あった] **If she were a boy, he would fight her.** もし彼女が男の子

だったら, 彼は彼女と取っ組み合いのけんかをしていただろう。《仮定法》

□ **what** 代①何が [を, に] ②~するところのもの [こと] ③なんと 形①何の, どんな ②なんと ③~するだけの 副いかに, どれほど

□ **when** 副①いつ ②~するところの, ~するそのとき, ~するとき 接~のとき, ~するとき 代①いつ ②そしてそのとき 名《the –》時, 場合

□ **where** 副①どこに [で] ②~するところの, そしてそこで, ~するところ 接~なところに [へ], ~するところに [へ] 代①どこ, どの点で ②~するところの 名《the –》場所

□ **which** 形①どちらの, どの, どれでも ②どんな~でも, そしてこの 代①どちら, どれ, どの人 [物] ②~するところの **on which** = when

□ **while** 接①~の間 (に), ~する間 (に) ②いっぽう, ~なのに 名しばらくの間, 一定の時 **after a while** しばらくして **for a while** しばらくの間

□ **white** 形白い, (顔色などが) 青ざめた, 白人の 名白, 白色

□ **who** 代①誰が [は], どの人 ②~するところの (人), するとその人は

□ **whose** 代①誰の ②(~の) …するところの

□ **why** 副①なぜ, どうして ②~するところの (理由) 間①おや, まあ ②もちろん, なんだって ③ええと

□ **wild** 形①野生の ②荒涼として ③荒っぽい, 乱暴な 副乱暴に, でたらめに

□ **will** 助~だろう, ~しよう, する (つもりだ) **Will you ~?** ~してくれませんか? 名決意, 意図 形《-ing》自発的な, 《be -ing to》喜んで~する

□ **Williams** 名ウィリアムズ《人名》

□ **Willie** 名ウィリー《人名》

□ **win** 動~に勝つ, ~を獲得する, ~に達する 名勝利, 成功

□ **wind** 名①風 ②うねり, 一巻き 動~を巻く, からみつく, うねる

□ **window** 名窓

□ **winter** 名冬

□ **wish** 動〜を望む［願う］，〜であればよいと思う《wish＋仮定法過去》主語＋wish（that）主語＋動詞過去〜 〜ならよいのに《wish＋仮定法過去完了》主語＋wish（that）主語＋動詞過去完了 〜 〜だったらよかったのに

□ **with** 前①《同伴・付随・所属》〜と一緒に，〜を身につけて，〜とともに ②《様態》〜（の状態）で，〜して ③《手段・道具》〜で，〜を使って

□ **without** 前〜なしで，〜がなく，〜しないで

□ **woke** 動wake（目がさめる）の過去

□ **woman** 名（成人した）女性，婦人

□ **women** 名woman（女性）の複数

□ **wonderful** 形驚くべき，すばらしい，すてきな

□ **won't** will not（〜しない［ではない］だろう）の短縮形

□ **wood** 名①《-s》森，林 ②木材

□ **word** 名①語，単語 ②ひと言 ③《one's –》約束 ④《the –》合い言葉

□ **wore** 動wear（〜を着ている，消耗する）の過去

□ **work** 動①働く ②機能［作用］する 名①仕事，勉強 ②職

□ **world** 名《the –》世界，界

□ **worry** 動悩む［悩ませる］，心配する［心配させる］ 名苦労，心配

□ **would** 動will（〜だろう）の過去 **would like to〜** 〜したいと思う **If she were a boy, he would fight her.** もし彼女が男の子だったら，彼は彼女と取っ組み合いのけんかをしていただろう。《仮定法》

□ **write** 動〜を書く，手紙を書く

□ **wrong** 形①間違った，(道徳上)悪い ②調子が悪い，故障した 副間違って 名不正，悪事

□ **wrote** 動write（〜を書く）の過去

Y

□ **yard** 名①庭，構内，仕事場 ②ヤード《長さの単位。約91cm》

□ **year** 名年，歳

□ **yellow** 形黄色の 名黄色

□ **yes** 副はい，そうです 名肯定の言葉［返事］

□ **yesterday** 名①昨日 ②過ぎし日，昨今 副昨日（は）

□ **yet** 副①《否定文で》まだ〜（ない［しない］） ②《疑問文で》もう ③《肯定文で》まだ，今もなお お 接それにもかかわらず，しかし，けれども

□ **you** 代①あなた（方）は［が］，あなた（方）を［に］ ②（一般に）人は

□ **young** 形若い，幼い，青年の

□ **your** 代あなた（方）の

□ **yours** 代あなた（方）のもの

□ **yourself** 代あなた自身

A
B
C
D
E
F
G
H
I
J
K
L
M
N
O
P
Q
R
S
T
U
V
W
X
Y
Z

[原著者]
マーク・トウェイン　Mark Twain
アメリカ近代文学の父とも呼ばれるマーク・トウェインは、1835年アメリカのミズーリ州で生まれた。若い頃は、印刷所の植字工見習い、蒸気船の水先案内人などをしながら暮らしを立て、その後、当時の体験や思い出から、『トム・ソーヤーの冒険』、『ハックルベリー・フィンの冒険』などの冒険小説を世に送り出した。

[リライト]
デイビッド・セイン　David Thayne
アメリカ出身。これまで累計350万部の著作を刊行してきた英語本のベストセラー著書。英会話学校経営、翻訳、英語書籍・教材制作などを行うクリエーター集団「エートゥーゼット」代表。日本で豊富な英語教授経験を持ち、これまで教えた日本人は数万人にのぼる。日本人に合った日本人のための英語マスター術を多数開発。英会話教育メソッド「デイビッド・セイン英語ジム」の監修も行っている。エートゥーゼット英語学校校長。

ラダーシリーズ

The Adventures of Tom Sawyer
トム・ソーヤーの冒険

2018年3月16日　第1刷発行
2022年2月11日　第3刷発行

原著者　マーク・トウェイン

発行者　浦　晋亮

発行所　IBCパブリッシング株式会社
　　　　〒162-0804 東京都新宿区中里町29番3号
　　　　菱秀神楽坂ビル9F
　　　　Tel. 03-3513-4511　Fax. 03-3513-4512
　　　　www.ibcpub.co.jp

© IBC Publishing, Inc. 2005

印刷　株式会社シナノパブリッシングプレス
装丁　伊藤 理恵　　本文イラスト　横井 智美
組版データ　Berkeley Oldstyle Medium + Palatino Italic

落丁本・乱丁本は、小社宛にお送りください。送料小社負担にてお取り替えいたします。本書の無断複写（コピー）は著作権法上での例外を除き禁じられています。

Printed in Japan
ISBN978-4-7946-0531-3